BEACONS

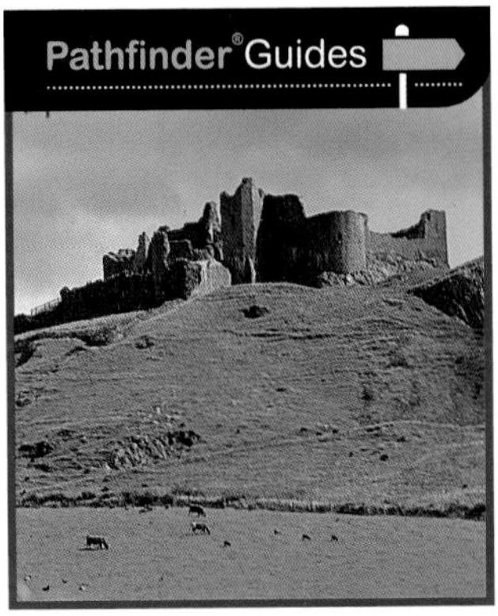

Outstanding Circular Walks

Originally compiled by
Brian Conduit and Neil Coates
Revised by Tom Hutton

Acknowledgements
Tom Hutton would like to thank all the staff of the Brecon Beacons National Park Authority and also his partner, Steph, for her company on many of the walks, and Du for her company on all of them – does she ever get tired?

Text:	Brian Conduit, Neil Coates, Tom Hutton Revised text for 2010 edition, Tom Hutton
Photography:	Brian Conduit and Tom Hutton
Editorial:	Ark Creative (UK) Ltd
Design:	Ark Creative (UK) Ltd

ISBN: 978-0-31909-001-5

While every care has been taken to ensure the accuracy of the route directions, the publishers cannot accept responsibility for errors or omissions, or for changes in details given. The countryside is not static: hedges and fences can be removed, field boundaries can alter, stiles can become gates, footpaths can be rerouted and changes in ownership can result in the closure or diversion of some concessionary paths. Also, paths that are easy and pleasant for walking in fine conditions may become slippery, muddy and difficult in wet weather, while stepping stones across rivers and streams may become impassable.

If you find an inaccuracy in either the text or maps, please write to Crimson Publishing at the address below.

First published 1993 by Jarrold Publishing
Revised and reprinted 1997, 2000, 2003, 2005, 2007

This edition first published in Great Britain 2010 by Crimson Publishing and reprinted with amendments in 2015 and 2016.

Crimson Publishing, 19-21C Charles Street, Bath, BA1 1HX

www.pathfinderwalks.co.uk

Printed in Spain by GraphyCems. 10/16

A catalogue record for this book is available from the British Library.

Front cover: Hay Bluff and the Gospel Pass
Previous page: Dramatic ruins of Carreg Cennen Castle

Contents

Approximate walk times

Up to 2½ hours
Short walks on generally clear paths

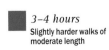

3–4 hours
Slightly harder walks of moderate length

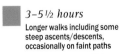

3–5½ hours
Longer walks including some steep ascents/descents, occasionally on faint paths

The walk times are provided as a guide only and are calculated using an average walking speed of 2½mph (4km/h), adding one minute for each 10m (33ft) of ascent, and then rounding the result to the nearest half hour.

Walks are considered to be dog friendly unless specified.

Keymap

Pont Llanio
Llanddewi Brefi
Llwyn-y-groes
Llangybi
Llanfair Clydogau
Cellan
Cwmann
Llanycrwys
Ffarmers
Cwrt-y-cadno
Ffaldybrenin
Pumsaint
Llandre
Caio
Crugybar
Llansawel
Edwinsford
Talley
Llansadwrn
Halfway
Cwmdu
Ashfield
Manordeilo
Salem
Cwmifor
Pen-y-banc
Rhosmaen
LLANDEILO
Ffairfach
Golden Grove
Trapp
Llandyfan
Milo
Carmel
Pentre-Gwenlais
Llandybie
Dre-fach
Saron
AMMANFORD
Betws
Pontamman
Garnant
Glanaman
Brynamman
Tycroes
Pantyffynnon
Greynor
Gwaun-Cae-Gurwen
Cwmgors
Tairgwaith
Cwmllynfell
Ystalyfera
Gurnos
Ystradgynlais
Cwmgiedd
Ystradowen
Cwm-twrch Uchaf
Cwm-twrch Isaf
Pontardawe
Rhyd-y-fro
Llangiwg
Cilmaengwyn
Clydach
Craig-cefn-parc
Pontarddulais
Hendy
Fforest
Felindre
Pontlliw
Llangennech
Bryn
Grovesend
Loughor
GORSEINON
Penllergaer
Llangyfelach
Morriston
Llansamlet
Gowerton
Waunarlwydd
Dunvant
Three Crosses
Killay
Upper Killay
Sketty
Landore
Fforest-fach
SWANSEA/ABERTAWE
Black Pill
West Cross
Bishopston
Newton
Pennard
Southgate
The Mumbles
Mumbles Head
Pwlldu Head
Oystermouth Castle
SWANSEA BAY
Kittle
Skewen
Birchgrove
Llandarcy
Glais
Bryn-coch
Rhydding
NEATH/CASTELL-NEDD
Tonna
Aberdulais
Cilfrew
Clyne
Resolven
Melincourt
Briton Ferry
Baglan
Cwmafan
Pontrhydyfen
PORT TALBOT
Taibach
Margam
Steel Works
Groes
Abbey
Eglwys Nunydd Reservoir
MAESTEG
Llangynwyd
Pont Rhyd-y-cyff
Coytrahên
Tondu
Bettws
Llangeinor
Blackmill
Bryncethin
Brynmenyn
Lewistown
Ogmore Vale
Ogmore Forest
Nant-y-moel
Price Town
Wyndham
Blaengarw
PONTYCYMER
Garth
Nantyffyllon
Caerau
Duffryn
Dyffryn
Croeserw
Abergwynfi
Blaengwynfi
Cymer
Glyncorrwg
TREORCHY
Cwmparc
Tynewydd
TREHERBERT
Blaenrhondda
Hirwaun
Hirwaun Common
Rhigos
Pontneddfechan
Glyn-neath
Morfa Glas
Blaengwrach
Cwmgwrach
Pentreclwydau
Crynant
Onllwyn
Seven Sisters
Dyffryn Cellwen
Coelbren
Caehopkin
Penrhos
Aber-craf
Ynyswen
Craig-y-nos
Pen-y-cae
Glyntawe
Penwyllt
Dan-yr-Ogof
Ystradfellte
Heol Senni
Cray
Sennybridge
Defynnog
Trecastle
Llywel
Halfway
Myddfai
Llangadog
Llanwrda
Cilgwyn
LLANDOVERY/LLANYMDDYFRI
Twynllanan
Llanddeusant
Capel Gwynfe
Bethlehem
Pant-Meredith
Felindre
Dyffryn Ceidrych
Porthyrhyd
Siloh
Cilycwm
Rhandirmwyn
Ystradffin
Cynghordy
Pentre-ty-gwyn
Babel
Llandeilo'r-Fan
Llanfihangel Nant Bran
Pentre-bach
Pentre'r-felin
Sugar Loaf Halt
LLANWRTYD WELLS
Llangammarch Wells
Cefn-gorwydd
Cwm Irton
Abergwesyn
Beulah
Tirabad
Gwryd
Blaendy
Bryn-du
Tywi Forest
Llyn Brianne Reservoir
Crychan Forest
Glasfynydd Forest
Usk Reservoir
BLACK MOUNTAIN
FFOREST FAWR
MYNYDD BWLCH-Y-GROES
ROMAN ROAD
Dyffryn Tywi
Swansea Valley
Vale of Neath
A40
A483
A482
A485
A4069
A474
A4068
A4067
A4221
A4109
A465
A4107
A4061
A4063
A4064
A48
M4
6
22
4
27
13
24

Keymap

SCALE 1:325 000 or 1 INCH to 5.2 MILES 1CM to 3.25 KM
0 2 4 6 8 10 KILOMETRES 15
0 2 4 6 MILES 8 10
SPOT HEIGHTS SHOWN IN METRES
BUILTH WELLS/ LLANFAIR-YM-MUALLT
HAY-ON-WYE
TALGARTH
BRECON/ ABERHONDDU
THE BLACK MOUNTAINS
BRECON BEACONS
BRECON BEACONS NATIONAL PARK
Crickhowell
ABERGAVENNY/ Y FENNI
BRYNMAWR
TREDEGAR
EBBW VALE
NANTYGLO
BLAENAVON
MERTHYR TYDFIL/ MERTHYR TUDFUL
RHYMNEY
ABERTILLERY
PONTYPOOL
USK
CWMBRAN
BLACKWOOD
CAERLEON
PONTYPRIDD
CAERPHILLY
NEWPORT/ CASNEWYDD
Offa's Dyke Path
River Wye
River Usk

Walk	Page	Start	Nat. Grid Reference	Distance	Time	Height Gain
Allt yr Esgair	26	Allt yr Esgair	SO 129226	3½ miles (5.6km)	2 hrs	950ft (290m)
The Blorenge	43	Keeper's Pond	SO 254107	6 miles (9.8km)	3 hrs	1,250ft (380m)
Brecon Beacons Horseshoe	88	Cwm Gwdi	SO 023247	8½ miles (13.7km)	5 hrs	2,890ft (880m)
Carn Goch	24	Carn Goch	SN 681242	3½ miles (4.8km)	2 hrs	820ft (250m)
Carreg Cennen	20	Carreg Cennen Castle	SN 666193	4 miles (6.4km)	2 hrs	590ft (180m)
Craig y Cilau & Llangattock	34	Craig y Cilau	SO 185168	5½ miles (8.8km)	3 hrs	1,115ft (340m)
Craig-y-nos, Cribath and the Henrhyd Falls	84	Craig-y-nos Country Park	SN 839155	8½ miles (13.7km)	4½ hrs	1,935ft (590m)
Cwm Oergwm	52	Llanfrynach	SO 074257	7 miles (11.3km)	3½ hrs	1,020ft (310m)
Cwmyoy	14	Cwmyoy Hall	SO 300226	2½ miles (4.2km)	1½ hrs	655ft (200m)
Fan y Big	77	Torpantau	SO 056175	10 miles (16.1km)	5½ hrs	2,000ft (610m)
Fan Fawr	46	Storey Arms Centre	SN 982203	4½ miles (7.3km)	3 hrs	1,325ft (405m)
Grwyne Fawr	70	Pont Cadwgan	SO 266251	7½ miles (12.1km)	4 hrs	1,720ft (525m)
Hay Bluff & Twmpa	58	Hay Bluff	SO 239373	6 miles (9.8km)	3 hrs	1,390ft (425m)
Llangors Lake	12	Llangors Lake	SO 128272	3½ miles (5.6km)	1½ hrs	130ft (40m)
Llangynidr & the River Usk	17	Llangynidr	SO 155195	3¾ miles (6km)	2 hrs	330ft (100m)
Llyn y Fan Fach and the Carmarthen Fans	66	Llanddeusant	SN 799238	6 miles (9.7km)	4 hrs	2,130ft (650m)
Monmouthshire & Brecon canal	28	Abergavenny	SO 299140	5½ miles (8.9km)	2½ hrs	330ft (100m)
Mynydd Illtud & Cefn Llechid	55	Mynydd Illtud	SN 977262	7½ miles (12.1km)	4 hrs	1,085ft (330m)
Mynydd Llangorse	30	Cockit Hill	SO 160283	5½ miles (8.9km)	3 hrs	1,115ft (340m)
Sugar Loaf	49	Llangenny	SO 239181	6 miles (9.7km)	3½ hrs	1,900ft (580m)
Table Mountain	32	Crickhowell	SO 218183	5 miles (8km)	3 hrs	1,250ft (380m)
Talgarth & Mynydd Troed	63	Talgarth	SO 152336	8 miles (13km)	4 hrs	1,050ft (320m)
Tor y Foel	37	Llangynidr	SO 146200	5½ miles (8.9km)	3 hrs	1,575ft (480m)
The Vale of Ewyas	60	Llanthony Priory	SO 289278	6 miles (9.7km)	3 hrs	1,210ft (370m)
Waterfalls Walk	73	Cwm Porth	SN 928124	9 miles (14.5km)	5 hrs	2,100ft (640m)
Waun Fach	80	Pengenffordd	SO 173296	7 miles (11.3km)	4½ hrs	2,200ft (670m)
Ysgyryd Fawr	22	Ysgyryd Fawr	SO 328164	2½ miles (4km)	2 hrs	960ft (315m)
Ystradfellte & Sarn Helen	40	Ystradfellte	SN 929134	6½ miles (10.4km)	3½ hrs	2,100ft (640m)

Comments
A steady climb through woodland leads to a superb viewpoint looking out over the Usk valley and Brecon Beacons.
A varied walk that starts high and crosses open hilltops before dropping to a nature reserve. The return leg climbs back onto the hilltops.
A long walk that embraces the three main peaks of the Brecon Beacons, including the highest point in southern Britain – sure to be immensely satisfying.
A short walk over impressive hill forts and rugged hillsides in the north west corner of the National Park.
The dramatically sited ruins of Carreg Cennen Castle, perched on its precipitous rock, are in sight for much of this walk.
A varied walk that includes woodland, an attractive stretch of canal, village and a dramatic limestone escarpment.
An energetic, varied and scenic walk that starts in an interesting country park and takes in a summit, a wooded gorge and a dramatic waterfall.
An energetic ramble deep into a lovely wooded valley that offers wonderful views over the high mountains above.
A short but quite steep walk that visits a magical village, complete with crooked church, and then climbs to a spectacular landmark with fine views.
A dramatic walk along the main escarpment of the Brecon Beacons is followed by a section along an ancient trackway and an attractive woodland finale.
A short but strenuous walk that climbs a gentle giant of a mountain with wonderful views over the central Brecon Beacons.
Conifer forest, open moorland and woodland provide plenty of variety, and an added bonus is a lovely secluded medieval church.
From the two most northerly peaks of the Black Mountains the panoramic views are superb. Expect some stiff climbing.
An easy walk mostly across flat, low lying meadows by Llangors Lake. There are some fine views across the lake.
An attractive walk that follows the mighty River Usk on the outward leg and the Brecon and Monmouthshire Canal on the return. Some very rough and slippery paths.
A strenuous but thoroughly invigorating walk that makes a brief foray into the wilderness of the Black Mountain, climbing two of its highest peaks and visiting a wonderful mountain lake.
A canal towpath and the track of a disused railway are utilised for this walk. There are fine views across the Usk valley to the distinctive Sugar Loaf.
Mostly open country with a wooded valley about halfway round, and for much of the way splendid views of the main range of the Brecon Beacons.
Grand views all the time on this enjoyable walk around Mynydd Llangorse, especially across Llangorse Lake to the line of the Brecon Beacons.
A wonderfully scenic walk that climbs from fertile valley floor to windswept mountaintop and back again.
A steady climb from Crickhowell to the top of Table Mountain rewards you with superb views over the Usk valley and surrounding mountains.
An interesting and varied ramble across pastures and onto open mountainsides, visiting an ancient long cairn on the return leg.
A short but quite steep walk over a distinctive mountain that offers wonderful views of the Brecon Beacons.
The steep-sided vale of Ewyas provides a superb setting for the beautiful, secluded ruins of Llanthony Priory, from which point this walk begins.
Wooded ravines and a series of spectacular waterfalls make for a fascinating walk. Expect some difficult paths and hard going in places.
Steady rather than strenuous climbing brings you to the highest point in the Black Mountains. The views from here are superb.
The climb to the summit of Ysgyryd Fawr is relatively easy but the views from it are outstanding. You return via the same gently sloping path.
There are expansive views across the austere landscape of Fforest Fawr and a fine stretch of Roman road.

Introduction to the Brecon Beacons

A glance at a map reveals two potential areas of confusion that need to be cleared up right from the start: what exactly is meant by 'the Brecon Beacons', and what is the relation between the Black Mountains and the Black Mountain? This possible confusion arises from the fact that within the boundaries of the Brecon Beacons National Park there are four separate mountain ranges. The most easterly is the Black Mountains, the Brecon Beacons themselves constitute only the central range despite giving their name to the whole area, to the west of them lies Fforest Fawr, and the most westerly range of all is the Black Mountain. For the remainder of this introduction 'Brecon Beacons' will be used for the national park as a whole and 'central Beacons' when referring specifically to the main central range.

The National Park has fairly clearly defined boundaries. In the east the most easterly ridges of the Black Mountains overlook the undulating country leading to the Wye Valley and the English border and at times slip over the border. The northern boundary is formed by the hills and moorlands of mid Wales and by the western reaches of the Usk Valley, before the River Usk bears south-eastwards to flow between the Black Mountains and the central Beacons. In the west the broad, lush vale of Towy makes an obvious boundary. But probably the most obvious boundary of all is to the south, although it is more of a historic, economic and environmental boundary: that between rural and industrial South Wales, largely marked by the line of the 'Heads of the Valleys' road between Abergavenny and Swansea.

Despite a basic similarity and uniformity of geology, each of the four ranges that constitute the Brecon Beacons has its own distinctive characteristics. The Black Mountains, the bulk of which lie to the west of the Wye and north of the Usk with a few detached 'outliers' around Abergavenny, comprise a series of long ridges separating narrow, quiet and still remote valleys. In the central Beacons a steep escarpment rises above the Usk Valley to a collection of smooth, rounded summits, the highest in the national park and including Pen-y-Fan 2,907 feet (886m), the highest point not only in South Wales but in the whole of southern Britain. Fforest Fawr, the 'Great Forest of Brecknock', was once a royal hunting ground, a bare, austere, lonely moorland area that lies between the upper reaches of the Taff to the east and the Tawe to the west. In the far west is the wildest and most remote area of the national park, the Black Mountain, brooded over by the bold and unmistakable profile of the Carmarthen Fans, Bannau Sir Gaer and Fan Brycheiniog.

The underlying unity of the Brecon Beacons as a whole comes from the area's basically simple geological structure. Most of it is underlain by Old Red Sandstone which gives it certain physical and scenic characteristics that distinguish it from the more rugged mountain areas of North Wales. This is an area of smooth, sweeping grassy uplands, wide and open vistas and, apart from the abrupt north-facing escarpment, gradual rather than steep or major gradients. The northern escarpment, caused by massive earth movements which thrust the mountains up and then tilted them to the south, is the most striking feature, stretching right across the region from the English border to the vale of Towy but seen at its most dramatic in the central Beacons and Black Mountain.

Only on the southern rim does the sandstone give way to overlapping bands of carboniferous rocks, limestone and millstone grit. Here can be found all the common features of carboniferous limestone scenery: scars, shake holes, gorges, caves, waterfalls and disappearing rivers. Particularly fascinating is the area south of Ystradfellte. Here limestone meets millstone grit, resulting in a series of spectacular falls on the rivers Mellte, Hepste, Neath and Pyrddin, the most concentrated area of waterfalls in Wales.

Youngest of the carboniferous rocks are the coal measures further south which gave rise to the mining industry and led to the tremendous industrial and population growth in the narrow, parallel valleys of the Rhymney, Taff, Dare and Rhondda which south extend like a series of fingers from the mountain core. At their southern end these coal-bearing valleys open out into the Vale of Glamorgan, an undulating limestone plateau ending in a dramatic line of cliffs on the Glamorgan coast.

The Brecon Beacons have their fair share of historic monuments. Prehistoric remains include stone circles, hill forts such as Crug Hywel above Crickhowell and Pen-y-crug above Brecon, and standing stones. Of the latter there are two particularly fine examples, Maen Llia and Maen Madoc, both of which have atmospheric locations, rising amid the lonely and austere moorlands of Fforest Fawr.

Both Roman and Norman conquerors avoided the mountain barrier to South Wales and took easier lowland routes, either to the north via the Usk Valley or to the south via the coast and the Vale of Glamorgan. The Romans have left little in the area apart from some well-preserved sections of road, notably Sarn Helen that runs across Fforest Fawr to the north of Ystradfellte and the 'Gap Road' through the central Beacons, although there is some doubt as to the Roman origins of the latter.

On the other hand, the Normans have left a chain of castles along their invasion routes to mark their line of conquest: Abergavenny, Crickhowell, Tretower, Bronllys and Brecon all fall within the park boundaries. One castle must be singled out as being particularly outstanding: Carreg Cennen, which is perched theatrically on a 300-feet (91m) high limestone crag in the foothills of the Black Mountain and is easily the most dramatically positioned castle in the National Park if not all of Wales.

The Normans also established monasteries around the fringes of the area. The most important of these were the Augustinian priory at Llanthony, beautifully situated in the secluded Vale of Ewyas deep in the Black Mountains, and the Benedictine priory at Brecon, elevated to cathedral status in 1923 and bestowing an added distinction on the principal town in the national park. Evidence of an older Celtic Christianity can be found in the fascinating little town of Llantwit Major near the Glamorgan coast, an important centre of learning during the Dark Ages.

Until the 19th century the region as a whole was a thinly populated farming area. By and large the Brecon Beacons area has remained that way, with just a few small villages and a number of pleasant market towns near the periphery of the National Park: Abergavenny, Hay-on-Wye, Crickhowell, Llandovery and Brecon. But the Industrial Revolution produced a virtual population explosion in the mining valleys to the south, as settlements sprang up along the steep valley sides and merged into each other to form a continuous urban development. The demand for high quality Welsh coal also led to the rapid expansion of Cardiff, which at the turn of the century was the world's greatest coal-exporting port, and the vast bulk of the population of Wales became concentrated in this south east corner of the country. In recent years the wheel has turned full circle. The mines have closed down, the waste tips have been landscaped and planted with trees, the valleys are becoming green again and the coal industry has started to recede into the area's heritage.

Although the Brecon Beacons largely escaped the ravages of the Industrial Revolution, the 20th century has had two major physical impacts on the area: the planting of conifer forests and the construction of reservoirs to serve the large towns and industrial areas to the south. Once regarded as alien intrusions in the landscape, they both now contribute to the region's tourist attractions. Nowadays tourism has become a vital part of the local economy.

The Brecon Beacons National Park has much to offer walkers. Apart from the obvious scenic attractions and walking challenges associated with any mountain area, there is a long tradition of *de facto* access to much of the open hillside and moorland. A further advantage is that much of the land, especially in the central Beacons, and including the highest peaks, is common land, owned either by the National Park or the National Trust.

A word of caution is needed, however. Because of their generally smooth and rounded appearance and the absence of craggy outlines, the Brecon Beacons may not look as daunting or formidable as the mountains of Snowdonia, the Lake District or the Scottish Highlands. But do not be misled. *These are true mountains which possess all the potential hazards of other mountain areas and need to be treated with due caution and respect. They have a high altitude and high rainfall, are subject to sudden mists – these are especially dangerous along the edge of the steep northern escarpment – and large areas of Fforest Fawr and the Black Mountain in the west comprise bare, trackless, featureless moorland.* Indeed, the area of the Carmarthen Fans in the Black Mountain is one of the few genuine areas of wilderness remaining in southern Britain and the National Park authorities are keen to preserve its unique quality of remoteness. Because of this, the walks in this book only scratch the surface of this area but experienced walkers might like to explore it for themselves, armed with the appropriate Ordnance Survey Explorer map.

For first time visitors the Brecon Beacons Mountain Centre near Libanus, to the south west of Brecon, is the ideal starting point. You can sit outside on the terrace admiring one of the most striking views in the whole of Wales, a panorama of the highest peaks in the Beacons, the core of the mountain massif. If that does not whet your appetite for exploring this beautiful, wild, fascinating area, nothing will.

This book includes a list of waypoints alongside the description of the walk, so that you can enjoy the full benefits of gps should you wish to. For more information on using your gps, read the *Pathfinder® Guide GPS for Walkers,* by gps teacher and navigation trainer, Clive Thomas (ISBN 978-0-7117-4445-5). For essential information on map reading and basic navigation, read the *Pathfinder® Guide Map Reading Skills* by outdoor writer, Terry Marsh (ISBN 978-0-7117-4978-8). Both titles are available in bookshops or can be ordered online at www.pathfinderwalks.co.uk

Glossary of Welsh Words

This list gives some of the more common elements in Welsh place names, which will allow readers to understand otherwise meaningless words and appreciate the relationship between place names and landscape features. Place names often have variant spellings, and the more common of these are given here.

aber	estuary, confluence
afon	river
bach, fach	small
bont, pont	bridge
bryn	mound, hill
bwlch	pass
caer	fort
capel	chapel
carn, carnedd	cairn
castell	castle
ceunant	gorge, ravine
coed	wood
craig	crag
crib	narrow ridge
cwm	valley
drws	doors, gap (pass)
dyffryn	valley
eglwys, llan	church
fach, bach	small
fawr, mawr	big
ffordd	road
foel, moel	rounded hill
glyn	glen
hen	old
llan, eglwys	church
llyn	lake
maen	stone
mawr, fawr	big
moel, foel	rounded hill
morfa	sea marsh
mynydd	mountain
nant	brook
newydd	new
pair	cauldron
pen	head, top
pont, bont	bridge
pwll	pool
rhaedr	waterfall
sarn	causeway
traeth	beach, shore
twll	hole
ynys	island

Llangors Lake

		GPS waypoints
Start	Llangors Lake	SO 128 272
Distance	3½ miles (5.6km)	Ⓐ SO 125 272
Height gain	130 feet (40m)	Ⓑ SO 122 263
Approximate time	1½ hours	Ⓒ SO 132 261
Parking	Free car park at Llangors Lake	Ⓓ SO 126 256
Route terrain	Mainly paths across level fields but a short section on a quiet road. Can get boggy and will flood at wetter times of year	Ⓔ SO 123 256
Dog friendly	Care needed on the road	
Ordnance Survey maps	Landranger 161 (The Black Mountains), Explorer OL13 (Brecon Beacons National Park – Eastern area)	

Llangors Lake, or Llyn Syfaddan, is the largest natural lake in South Wales and is noted for its rich flora and fauna, especially bird life. For much of this flat, easy, relaxing walk around its shores the lake is hidden but from time to time lovely views open up across the water to Mynydd Llangorse. After wet weather the low-lying and badly drained meadows bordering the lake are likely to be waterlogged.

From the car park walk straight across the field beside it, looking out for a waymarked footbridge over the Afon Llynfi. The whole of this walk is well waymarked and easy to follow. Cross the bridge Ⓐ, turn half-left and head across a meadow to a gate at the far end. Continue across a series of meadows, going through a succession of gates and curving gradually to the left all the while. Llangors Lake is to the left and there are fine views of Mynydd

Looking across Llangors Lake

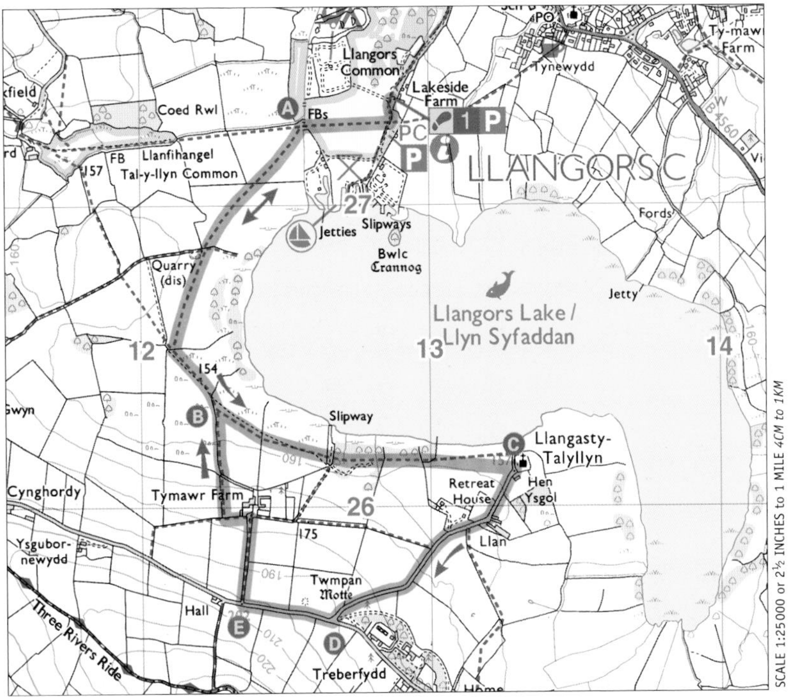

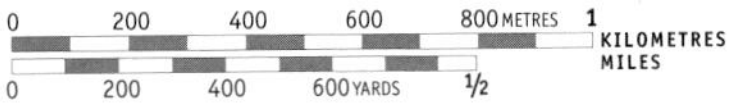

Llangorse and Allt yr Esgair.

On reaching a waymarked post where paths meet B, keep straight ahead to walk along the edge of the field, with the lake to your left, to a gate in the corner of a wood. This leads onto a track that veers leftwards to a hide. The walk continues right then left to continue in the same direction with the wood on the left. This soon leads you to a boardwalk, which you follow around the edge of the woodland, and this eventually leads out onto another meadow, where you'll see Llangasty-Talyllyn church ahead. There are also lovely views across the lake.

Go through a gate just to the left of the church C and turn right along a track which bears right to continue as a tarmac lane through the hamlet. The church, school and manor house at Llangasty-Talyllyn were all built in the middle of the 19th century for Robert Raikes, the founder of the Sunday School movement, to form a religious community. Follow the lane for ½ mile, heading gently uphill to a T-junction D. Turn right, in the Pennorth direction, and continue for another ¼ mile to a farm drive on the right, signed to Ty-Mawr Camping E. Turn right and walk down a tarmac track towards a farm. Just in front of the farm buildings turn left over a stile, walk along the right-hand edge of a field, by a hedge on the right, and turn right over the next stile.

Head gently downhill along the left-hand edge of a field, by a hedge on the left, climb a stile in the field corner, cross an enclosed path and climb another stile immediately ahead. Bear left to continue down the left-hand edge of a meadow to a waymarked post B and a gate just beyond. At the post pick up the outward route and retrace your steps to the start. ●

Cwmyoy

Start	Cwmyoy Hall
Distance	2½ miles (4.2km)
Height gain	655 feet (200m)
Approximate time	1½ hours
Parking	Cwmyoy Hall, on minor road along the Vale of Ewyas
Route terrain	A mixture of easy paths across fields and steep rocky tracks
Ordnance Survey maps	Landranger 161 (The Black Mountains), Explorer OL13 (Brecon Beacons National Park – Eastern area)

GPS waypoints

- Start: SO 300 226
- A: SO 300 231
- B: SO 299 233
- C: SO 298 235
- D: SO 297 238
- E: SO 301 237

Not many small villages draw quite as much attention as Cwmyoy. Its medieval church is so crooked it's difficult to find a truly upright wall, and the village itself is perched precariously on a steep hillside dominated by a craggy knoll. This walk crosses gently sloping meadows to reach the village, and from the church climbs steeply above the houses, for some staggering views of the surrounding valleys. If the steep pull looks too much, the walk can be shortened by going only as far as the church and then returning by the same route.

Parking is extremely limited in the village of Cwmyoy itself, so the best starting point for this walk is outside Cwmyoy Hall on the other side of the Afon Honddu on the minor road that runs through the Vale of Ewyas. If these spaces are all taken, there is further parking about 1½ miles down the valley.

Start: With your back to the hall, turn right onto the road and walk past a cottage to a stile on the right. Cross this and walk down through the field to a gate ahead. Go through and bear left to follow a faint path to a footbridge over the Afon Honddu, and then continue ahead through the small copse to emerge at the foot of a long field. Walk up the left-hand edge of the field with fine views all around, and continue to a stile at the top that leads out onto a lane (A).

Y Craig and St Martin's Church

Turn left here and walk past a farm on the left to a sharp right-hand bend. Continue around this, ignoring a turning on the left, and pass a telephone box on your left before continuing uphill past an old millstone in the wall on the left. Now go around a sharp left-hand bend and you'll see St Martin's Church directly ahead. Continue towards this, passing through a small gate and following an inscribed flagstone path to the main entrance **B**.

The building itself is really quite surreal with barely a true right angle anywhere in its construction. The tower leans at a quite incredible angle and parts of the main wall seem to almost bulge outwards – caused by movements in the underlying rock rather than shoddy workmanship. From the inside it's equally impressive and even the headstones on the surrounding graves lean at various different angles.

It's possible to shorten the walk and avoid a steep and rough climb by retracing your steps back to Cwmyoy Hall from here.

Now follow the path that leads uphill from the church, and go through the gate at the top onto another lane. Turn left for a few paces and then turn right at a waymark to Graig. Climb steeply up the sunken track to a gate at the top and go through this to a junction of paths, by a Hatherall Hill interpretation board **C**. Turn left to follow the broad path along beneath a spectacularly positioned wooden cabin to a gate. Go through this and keep straight ahead on a narrow path that follows a bank and a line of trees, and later a wall. Continue for 200 yds to a junction with a track on the right, above the buildings of Darren Isaf **D**, and turn sharp right onto this to climb steeply up towards the craggy knoll above. Aim to the right of a lone tree and then follow the wall on the right to a stile in the field corner. Cross this into the open access land beyond, and if you've the energy you can scramble up the steep narrow path on the right to the top, where there are wonderful views of the Vale of Ewyas and surrounding mountains. From the stile turn half left to follow a narrow path down through the bracken with a wall to the left. Go past a deep notch in

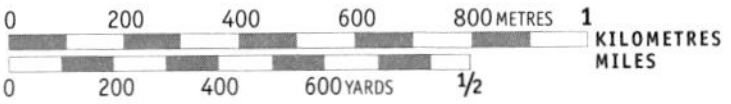

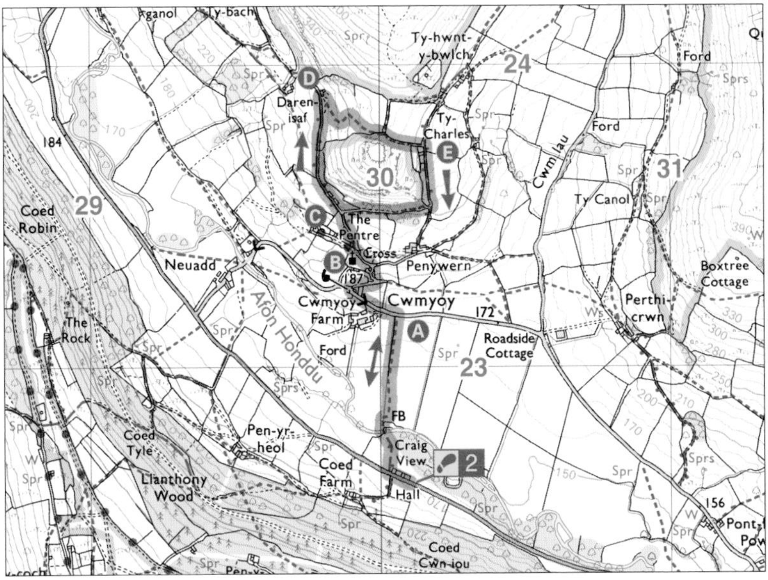

SCALE 1:25 000 or 2½ INCHES to 1 MILE 4CM to 1KM

the crags to the right and continue as the track then widens and drops by a wall to a T-junction Ⓔ, where you should turn right to pass beneath a house. Continue with a fence on the right and when this ends, ignore a stile straight ahead and instead turn right to follow the clear path back to the junction of paths by the interpretation board.

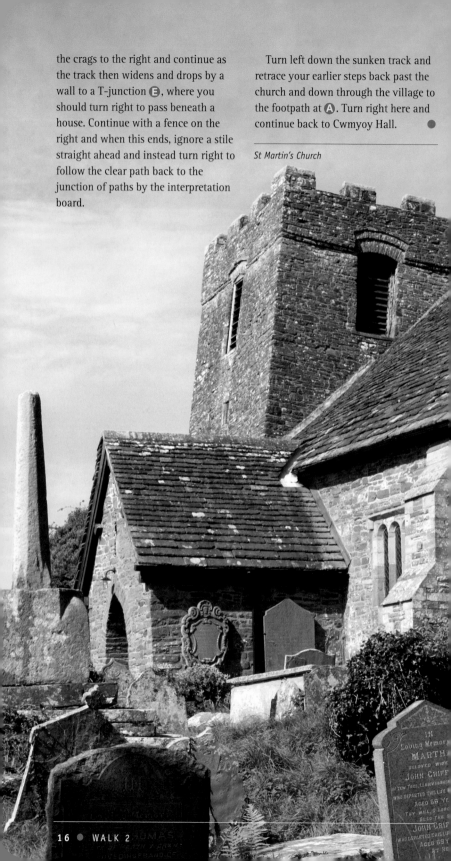

Turn left down the sunken track and retrace your earlier steps back past the church and down through the village to the footpath at Ⓐ. Turn right here and continue back to Cwmyoy Hall. ●

St Martin's Church

Llangynidr and the River Usk

Start	Llangynidr, main car park
Distance	$3\frac{3}{4}$ miles (6km)
Height gain	330 feet (100m)
Approximate time	2 hours
Parking	Llangynidr Community Car Park (free)
Route terrain	A mixture of rough rocky paths and a well-surfaced canal towpath
Dog friendly	A couple of awkward stone stiles
Ordnance Survey maps	Landranger 161 (The Black Mountains), Explorer OL13 (Brecon Beacons National Park – Eastern area)

GPS waypoints

- (start) SO 155 195
- Ⓐ SO 165 198
- Ⓑ SO 158 202
- Ⓒ SO 152 202
- Ⓓ SO 145 200
- Ⓔ SO 146 198
- Ⓕ SO 160 197

The River Usk begins high on the grassy uplands of the Mynydd Du, in the far west of the National Park. By the time it starts to meander southwards, it has become a magnificent waterway; wide and wild, with cataracts and rapids at almost every turn. As it approaches the village of Llangynidr, it starts to run parallel to the Brecon and Monmouthshire Canal, making it possible to link rough riverbank footpaths with the canal towpath to make a rewarding short circular walk.

Walk out of the small gate at the end of the car park and turn right onto the main road. Then turn straight away left, down Cyffredyn Lane and follow this down, over a bridge over the Brecon and Monmouthshire canal, which provides your return route.

Continue along the lane until you round a sharp right-hand bend, where you'll see a waymarked, walled footpath leading left. Follow this down to the River Usk Ⓐ and turn left to walk along the bank, on a sandy and sometimes rocky path. Cross a stile and continue in the same direction across a meadow, with great views down over the river.

Continue in the same direction now, crossing a succession of stiles and taking great care on a few rocky sections that can be very slippery when wet. After ½ mile the path turns slightly away from the riverside to pass an impressive waterfall Ⓑ. Stay with it as it drops back down again and keep ahead for another ½ mile and you'll come to a tarmac drive, with a gate ahead marked Pen Isha Coed. Walk up to the gate and then turn right infront of it to locate a narrow path that continues with bushes to the right, and a fence to the left. Keep ahead until you reach the road next to Llangynidr Bridge Ⓒ. This magnificent structure,

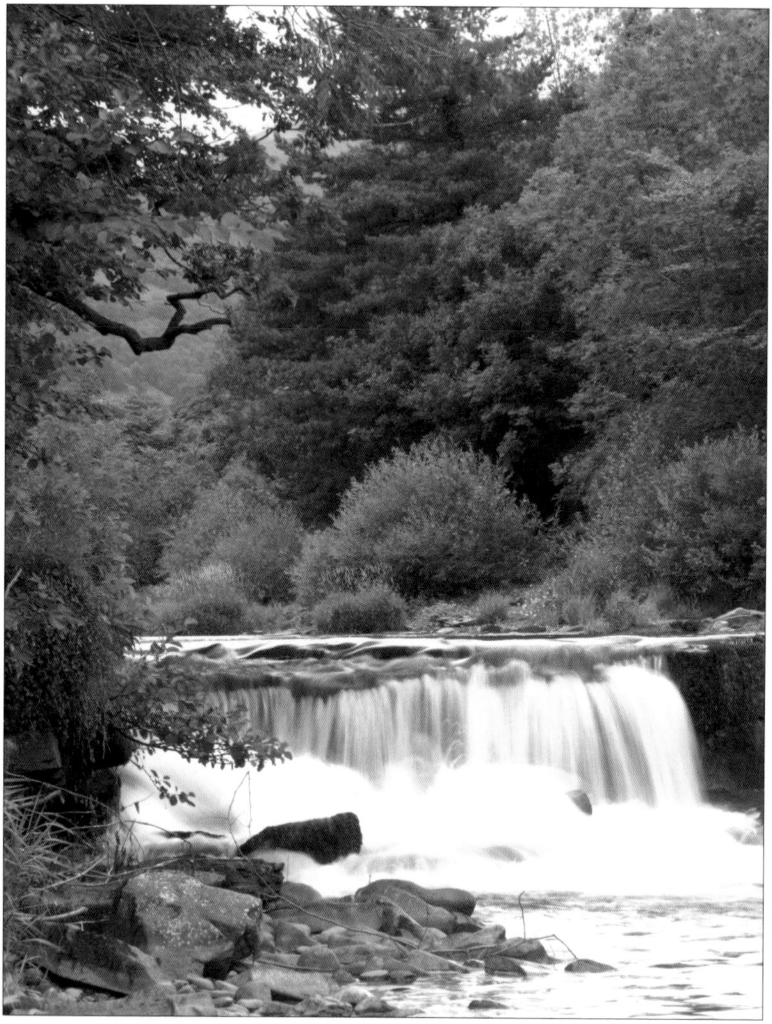

River Usk near Llangynidr

which spans the River Usk just north of the village, was originally built between 1587 and 1630, and would have originally carried packhorses, hence its narrow profile and the need for quite severe traffic restrictions.

Cross the road and follow the waymarked footpath straight ahead. It runs behind gardens for a short distance and then drops down to the banks of the river again. Now continue upstream, first in woods and later with better views. Ignore a path that leads up left, marked with a red-topped post and continue for a few more paces, where a set of steps leads away from the river for a final time **D**.

Turn right at the top, and follow the narrow drive up to a road that runs alongside the canal, by a lock. There are five locks at Llangynidr, which were actually constructed to a slightly unusual size, but as the canal had no links with any other canal system, this did not really cause a problem. Turn right here to follow the road into Llangynidr for refreshments in the **Coach and Horses**, which you'll see to the left **E**.

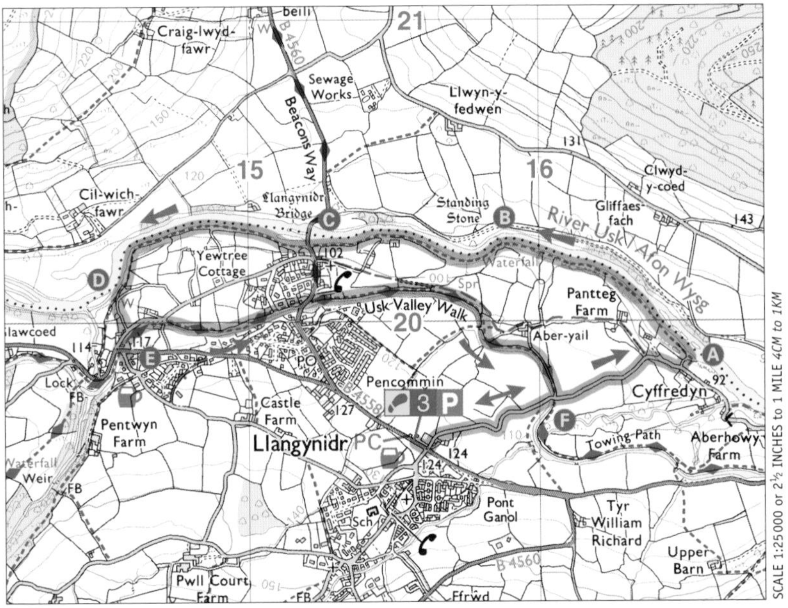

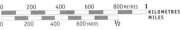

There's a fine viaduct over the Afon Crawnon, just a few paces farther along the canal from the main road.

If you do not want to visit the village, bear left, with the lock to your right, and follow the canal towpath easily eastwards. This is a good place to spot kingfishers, which can usually be heard before they are seen. You'll soon pass beneath a bridge, where the waterway runs under the B4560, a few yards above Llangynidr Bridge. You'll now need to walk beneath one more bridge before finally leaving the canal by a stile on the left, just before you reach another (No. 129) F. This rejoins Cyffredyn Lane, where you need to turn right to retrace your steps back up into the village and the car park. ●

Lock on the Brecon and Monmouthshire Canal

Carreg Cennen

Start	Carreg Cennen Castle
Distance	4 miles (6.4km)
Height gain	590 feet (180m)
Approximate time	2 hours
Parking	Free car park at Carreg Cennen
Route terrain	Mainly clear paths across sheep pasture and through deciduous woodland
Dog friendly	No dogs in castle grounds and many awkward stiles
Ordnance Survey maps	Landranger 159 (Swansea & Gower), Explorer OL12 (Brecon Beacons National Park – Western area)

GPS waypoints

Start	SN 666 193
A	SN 666 188
B	SN 671 177
C	SN 673 180
D	SN 675 192

The major attraction of this popular and well-waymarked walk in the western foothills of the Black Mountain is the ever-changing views of Carreg Cennen Castle, perched on its precipitous rock, from many different angles. The finale is superb – a steady ascent through woodland to the castle entrance.

One of the most dramatically sited castles in Britain, Carreg Cennen occupies a 300 feet (91m) - high exposed vertical limestone outcrop above the Cennen valley. It is everyone's idea of what a ruined castle should be like; it is even complete with an underground passage, hewn from the rock, which leads down into a cave. Originally a Welsh fortress, stronghold of the Lords Rhys, it was taken by the English and rebuilt and strengthened in the late 13th and early 14th centuries. Most of its extensive remains belong to that period.

At the far end of the car park go through a gate into the farmyard of Castle Farm. Do not continue ahead between the farm buildings towards the castle, but turn right just before the house to walk across a gravel area to a gate. Head downhill across a field, making for a stile and footpath sign in the bottom left-hand corner – like most of the signs on this walk it has a castle symbol on it. Climb the stile and turn left along a narrow lane.

Ignore the first stile on the right and follow the lane downhill, curving left to a second stile just before a cottage, at a public footpath sign to Llwyn-bedw **A**. Turn right over the stile, head downhill across a field, bearing slightly right to climb a stile in the field corner, and continue along a steep downhill path to climb another stile at the bottom. Go across the next field, cross a footbridge over the River Cennen and bear slightly left to head uphill to a stile. Climb it and continue steeply uphill, keeping parallel with a wire fence and line of trees on the left, towards a farm. Turn right at the top, before the buildings and continue beyond them before going through a gap in the hedge to join a drive. Turn right on to this and follow it easily away from the farm, through an area of scattered trees. After fording a stream, the track bends to the right and then curves left to reach a footpath sign a few yards ahead.

Turn left here over a stile and walk along a track, by a hedge bank on the right, bearing slightly left to cross a footbridge over a narrow stream and continuing to a stile. Climb it and bear slightly right along an enclosed track; this later emerges briefly into a more open area before continuing as a tree-lined route by the infant River Loughor on the right, a most attractive part of the walk. Climb a stile and if you want to see the source of the Loughor which issues from a cave here, another stile immediately to the right gives access.

Continue along the track, which curves slightly left and winds gently uphill, by a wire fence on the right. It then turns left to continue initially by a hedge bank on the right, and later veers left away from it to a stile. Climb the stile, bear right to pass between two hollows and head across to climb a stile onto a lane **B**.

Turn left, climb a stile beside a cattle-grid and continue along the lane as far as a right-hand bend **C**. Here keep ahead along a track, by a wire fence and hedge bank on the right. To the right are the Pillow Mounds – artificial rabbit warrens made by local people in the 19th century to ensure a regular supply of fresh meat. As the track curves right to the house, keep left to cross a stile and follow the waymarked path along with a fence to the left. This eventually swings right and becomes fenced on both sides as it heads towards the brow of a hill. Continue over the hill and down again to a stile that leads onto a sunken track. Follow this down to join a broad track at a hairpin bend and turn left to take the lower track, and then, as the track turns sharply left, bear right to cross a stile and drop down a stony, tree-and hedge-lined path, climbing another stile and keeping by a stream on the right. Turn right to cross a footbridge over the stream, turn left along the other bank, climb a stile and keep ahead to cross another footbridge over the River Cennen **D**.

Turn right and almost immediately turn sharp left, at a footpath sign to Carreg Cennen, onto a path that heads steadily uphill through the lovely, sloping Coed y Castell (Castle Wood) towards the castle. Continue past the castle entrance at the top and follow the path as it descends, turning right through a kissing-gate, on through another one and down through Castle Farm to return to the start. ●

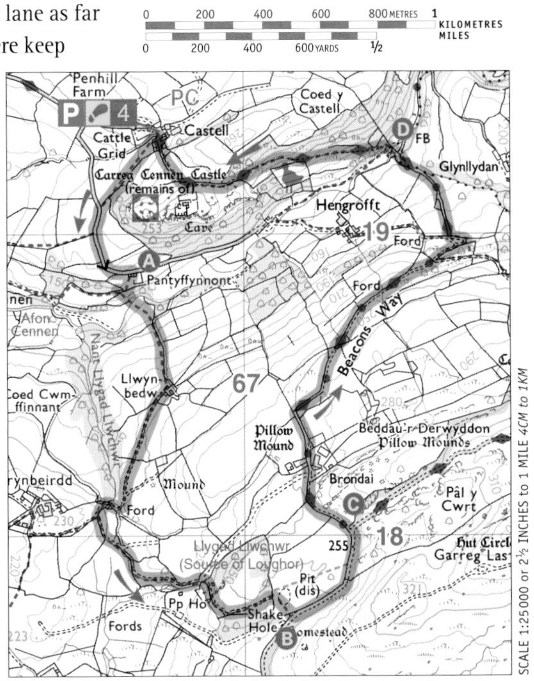

Ysgyryd Fawr

		GPS waypoints
Start	Ysgyryd Fawr	(start) SO 328 164
Distance	2½ miles (4km)	A SO 327 166
Height gain	960 feet (315m)	B SO 327 169
Approximate time	2 hours	C SO 331 182
Parking	National Park free car park on B4521 between Abergavenny and Skenfrith	
Route terrain	Well marked paths through woodland followed by a deer path along a narrow ridge. Some steep ground	
Ordnance Survey maps	Landranger 161 (The Black Mountains), Explorer OL13 (Brecon Beacons National Park – Eastern area)	

The distinctive bulk of Ysgyryd Fawr, alternatively called the Skirrid or Holy Mountain, lies to the north east of Abergavenny and is the most easterly detached outlier of the Black Mountains. Its 'holy' connections derive from its shape: various legends claim that the cleft in its ridge was created either by Noah's Ark or at the time of the Crucifixion, but the more prosaic explanation is that it was the result of a massive landslip. The walk to its summit, a steep climb initially through woodland and later along an open, grassy, narrow ridge, gives splendid views in all directions. Although it is possible to descend from the summit to a path that encircles the hill, the northern slopes are so steep that it is better to return by the same route used on the ascent, with the opportunity to enjoy the fine views again from a different angle.

Approaching the summit of Ysgyryd Fawr

Start by walking around the barrier at the side of the car park, and walk along the track, which soon bends around to the right and climbs gently between hedges to reach a double gate with a stile on its left. Climb over the stile and walk past a bench and up the forest track for another 20 yds to a turning on the right **A**, marked by a short post with an arrow on the top. Follow this path upwards, soon

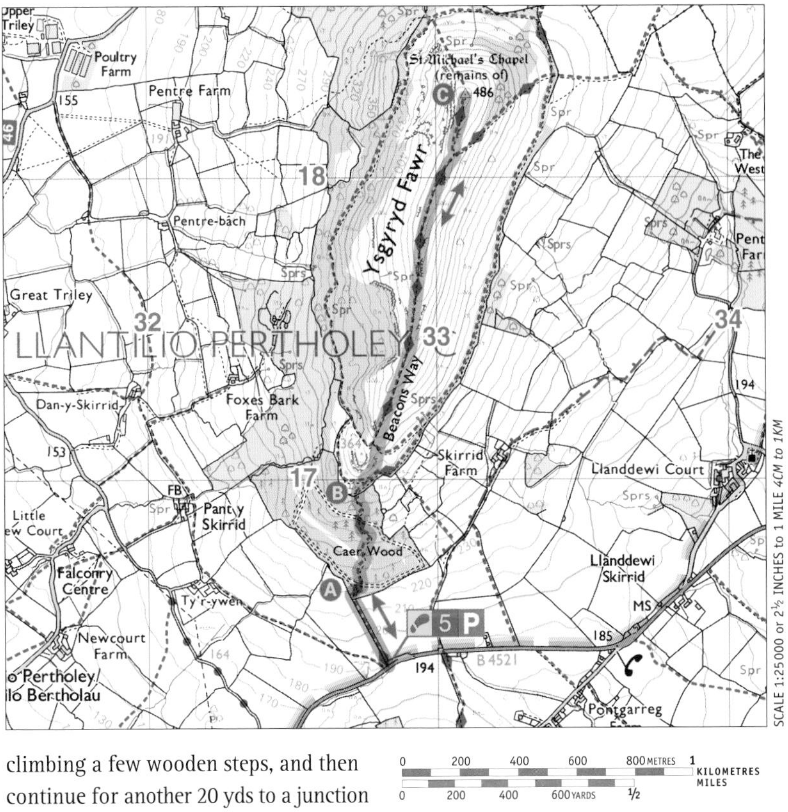

climbing a few wooden steps, and then continue for another 20 yds to a junction with another broad forest track. Keep straight ahead to cross this and continue upwards on a broad footpath that is again marked by a small post on the right.

This section of path is a lot longer than the previous one, continuing deep into the woods. Stay with it and eventually you'll emerge onto another forest track, which you cross again to continue the climb. Follow the path upwards again and you'll soon come to a large gate, with a walker's gate to the right of it **B**.

Go through the gate and turn right to walk along a level path, with a wall to your right. Continue for 100 yds and turn left onto a path that can be seen winding up the hillside.

The path continues quite steeply uphill, eventually emerging onto a small, open grassy area. Turn sharp right, shortly turn left to follow a well-worn path up to the ridge, and continue along the ridge to the triangulation pillar at the summit **C**. The walk along this narrow, grassy ridge is most enjoyable, a gradual and easy climb with magnificent views on both sides. The finest views of all are from the summit (1,595 feet/486m): a great arc takes in Abergavenny, the Usk Valley, Blorenge, the Sugar Loaf, the Black Mountains, and the more gentle countryside to the east looking towards the English border and the Wye and Monnow valleys. In the Middle Ages a chapel was built here for the pilgrims who were attracted by the hill's religious connections but it is virtually impossible to see any traces of it now.

From the summit retrace your steps to the start. ●

Carn Goch

Start	Carn Goch
Distance	3½ miles (4.8km)
Height gain	820 feet (250m)
Approximate time	2 hours
Parking	Free parking area on narrow lane that leads south from Bethlehem
Route terrain	A mix of paths over farmland and rough mountainside
Ordnance Survey maps	Landrangers 159 (Swansea & Gower) and 160 (Brecon Beacons), Explorer OL12 (Brecon Beacons National Park – Western area)

GPS waypoints

- (start) SN 681 242
- A SN 690 243
- B SN 696 242
- C SN 692 228
- D SN 688 228
- E SN 681 234

Situated in the far north west corner of the National Park, Carn Goch is one of the largest and most impressive hill forts in Wales. It's actually two hill forts in one: Y Gaer Fach (the small fort) and Y Gaer Fawr (the large fort), which are positioned on adjacent hilltops high above the Twyi Valley. The name Carn Goch translates to the Red Cairn and likely a reference to the huge burial cairn that crowns the larger fort. The land is owned and maintained by the National Park Authority. This walk links an exploration of the two hill forts with the hills to the south, which rise higher but are somehow not quite as impressive. It finishes easily, first dropping through sheep pasture and then following a narrow lane.

(start) From the left-hand end of the parking area, take the clear path that leads behind the interpretation signs and follow it steadily uphill, passing an impressive standing stone that is in fact a memorial to Plaid Cymru MP Gwynfor Evans, and despite its authentic appearance was actually erected in July 2006. Continue to the top where you cross a bank of stones – the smaller fort's western ramparts. Keep ahead; still following a vague path and you'll drop past another bank of stones, the eastern ramparts, onto the broad saddle that divides the two hilltops.

Stay with the path to cross this saddle, then climb up onto the earthworks that once protected the western end of Y Gaer Fawr. Turn sharp left when you reach the top and follow a steep and stony ramp up through the ramparts onto easier ground. Now keep straight ahead towards the huge cairn **A**. The views from this section are quite breathtaking and it's easy to see how well-protected the fort would have been in such an imposing position.

Keep the giant cairn to your left and drop into a hollow with a grassy ridge to your right. Head towards the far end of this ridge where a gap in the stone ramparts leads out onto a rough but gentle slope. Bear half right to follow a vague track down across the hill, eventually reaching the road opposite the drive to Tan-y-lan Farm Ⓑ. Turn right onto the road and as you approach Garn Wen Farm, keep left to cross a stile that leads onto a narrow path with the house up and to the right.

Follow this through a gate, where it broadens and then keep straight ahead climbing up through further gates to a small square field, where you turn left to a junction with another track, and then turn right onto it, to continue in the same direction. At the next gate, turn right to follow the field edge to a stile and cross this and keep to the left hand, top edge of the field to pass through a gap in the wall on your left to another stile Ⓒ.

Cross this into woodland and keep ahead to gradually drop down to join a broad track at the bottom. Turn right to go through a gate, and then turn left to drop to a stile Ⓓ. Cross this and continue down the tree-lined track, which follows the line of a stream. Keep straight ahead, crossing a succession of stiles and trying to keep to the easiest and driest ground and you'll eventually cross a stile that leads into an open field.

Keep straight ahead to the bottom of this and then continue with the row of trees to your right, bearing half left at the bottom of this field to cross another stile. Now follow a marker post diagonally across the field towards a wall corner and then deflect slightly left again to drop to a gate Ⓔ.

Turn right onto the road and follow it past Cwmdu Cottage and around to the left. Drop to cross a bridge and then continue to a junction, where you turn right. Now follow this lane easily back to the cattle-grid by the car park, where you turn right to finish. ●

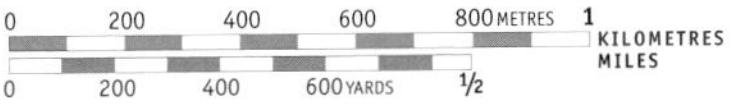

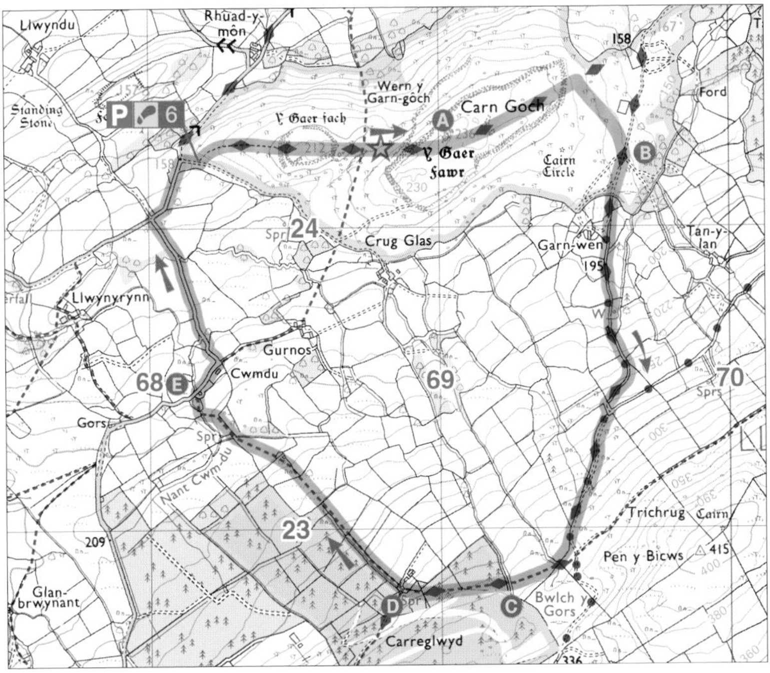

SCALE 1:25000 or 2½ INCHES to 1 MILE 4CM to 1KM

Allt yr Esgair

Start	Allt yr Esgair
Distance	3½ miles (5.6km)
Height gain	950 feet (290m)
Approximate time	2 hours
Parking	Free car park and picnic area off A40 ½ mile south of Llansantffraed
Route terrain	Wooded paths, steep and occasionally muddy in places, and a short section that crosses an open hilltop
Ordnance Survey maps	Landranger 161 (The Black Mountains), Explorer OL13 (Brecon Beacons National Park – Eastern area)

GPS waypoints

- SO 129 226
- Ⓐ SO 123 251
- Ⓑ SO 131 231

Allt yr Esgair is a narrow, wooded ridge that lies between the Usk Valley and Llangorse Lake. From its highest slopes there are extensive views and attractive woodland clothes its lower slopes. There is plenty of climbing but none is too steep or strenuous.

Begin by going through a gate beside the car park, at a public bridleway sign to Allt yr Esgair, onto an enclosed track, and almost immediately turn left through a metal gate. Head diagonally uphill across two fields, go through a gate and continue uphill in the same direction to enter an attractive wooded area. All the way there are fine views through the trees to the left across the Usk Valley to the Brecon Beacons. Go through a gate and continue through the woodland, to climb steadily to reach a track.

The Brecon Beacons from Allt yr Esgair

Turn left along this lovely, grassy, fairly flat track which keeps along the left-hand edge of woodland; below on the left Llansantffraed church and the village of Talybont-on-Usk can be seen. Continue through another gate and keep ahead, staying on the main track, to eventually join another track at a waymark post. Keep left onto this, waymarked Penorth, to continue in the same direction, and go through a succession of gates, passing the ruined Paragon Tower, an early 19th-century hunting lodge, on the right. Keep ahead along a narrow path that winds through gorse, trees, bracken and rough grass; keeping roughly in the same direction the whole time. When it emerges into an open meadow walk straight ahead across it, bearing right at the far end into trees above a covered reservoir. In front is a superb view of Llangorse Lake backed by Mynydd Llangorse.

Once in the trees, turn sharp right Ⓐ onto a path marked 'Pedestrians only' that leads steeply up through brambles and gorse. The path, sunken and enclosed in places, heads quite steeply uphill, eventually merging with the path for horses and cyclists, and following a dry stone wall up onto the open hilltop, by some large rocks. Here is the finest view of all, over the Usk Valley to the Brecon Beacons

Keep ahead, and descend to a gate, then continue to the right of a plantation to a fork. Bear right towards a wall corner and then continue with the wall to your left and a fence to your right. Keep ahead through another gate and drop down through a meadow to another gate. Go through this onto a tree-lined track and take the first turning on the right Ⓑ. Follow this down until it bends to the right and heads down to a farm.

Just before reaching the farm, turn sharp left, waymarked A40, and go through a gate to a T-junction of paths, where you turn right. A few yards ahead turn left (not sharply left through a metal gate) down an enclosed, stony, sunken, tree-lined path. Go through a gate and continue down to go through another gate to return to the start. ●

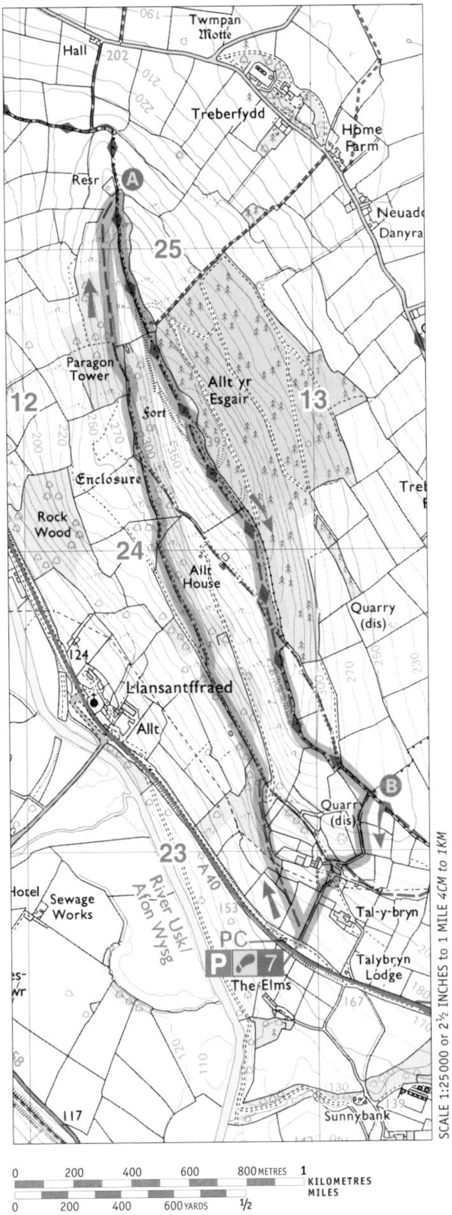

The Monmouthshire and Brecon Canal

Start	Abergavenny Castle
Distance	5½ miles (8.9km)
Height gain	330 feet (100m)
Approximate time	2½ hours
Parking	Nearby Byfield Road car park, fee on Tuesdays
Route terrain	Good paths across riverside meadows, canal towpaths and well-surfaced disused railway line. Crosses a busy road
Dog friendly	Care needed on the road
Ordnance Survey maps	Landranger 161 (The Black Mountains), Explorer OL13 (Brecon Beacons National Park – Eastern area)

GPS waypoints

Start	SO 299 140
A	SO 291 139
B	SO 287 138
C	SO 286 132
D	SO 285 130
E	SO 268 137

As most of this walk is either across riverside meadows, along a canal towpath or along the track of a disused railway, it is bound to be easy and relaxing. The sections along the banks of the River Usk and the towpath of the Monmouthshire and Brecon Canal are especially attractive and there are some fine views over the Usk Valley to the Sugar Loaf and Ysgyryd Fawr.

Encircled by the outlying hills of the Black Mountains Abergavenny guards one of the main routes into the heart of South Wales, a position appreciated by the Norman conquerors, who built the castle. In the Middle Ages Abergavenny Castle was one of the main border strongholds, but nowadays little remains and the 'keep' is a 19th-century imitation. Abergavenny lies on the eastern edge of the National Park and makes an excellent walking centre.

The walk begins at the entrance to the castle grounds. Facing the entrance, turn right and head down the lane beside the castle walls. After about 100 yds the lane ends and ahead are two paths; take the right-hand, lower, one which descends by a wall on the right, and turn right at the bottom onto a paved path. Pass through a gate and continue across a meadow to reach the bank of the River Usk. Ahead is a grand view of Blorenge.

Turn right onto another paved path that follows the river along to Usk Bridge **A**, turn left over the bridge and immediately turn right onto a lane, which is a footpath that leads to the cemetery. The lane passes to the right of the cemetery and then swings left B, downhill, to pass through a tunnel that leads beneath the Heads of the Valleys Road. Continue past a garden centre and uphill slightly to meet the road on the outskirts of Llanfoist village, close to the Llanfoist Crossing car park C.

Cross the road and continue up the lane ahead, which is signposted 'Blorenge and Usk Valley Walk', passing to the right of Llanfoist church and heading steadily uphill between trees. At a fork bear right to an aqueduct but just before reaching it turn right up steps to join the canal towpath D. Turn right to follow the towpath for 1½ miles by the tree-fringed, tranquil waters of the canal, high above the Usk Valley with fine views to the right over Abergavenny and the Sugar Loaf, and below the steep, thickly wooded lower slopes of Blorenge on the left. The canal was built between 1797 and 1812 to provide a link between Brecon and the Bristol Channel and carried coal, iron, lime and agricultural produce. After the inevitable decline and fall into disuse, it was restored and reopened in 1970 as a recreational waterway.

At the first bridge turn left over the canal and turn right to walk along the other bank, passing under a second bridge and continuing past a marina by Govilon Boat Club. At a third bridge E climb steps to leave the canal and turn right along the track of a disused railway, part of a line built in the 1860s to link the coal mines around Merthyr Tydfil, Tredegar and Ebbw Vale to the Monmouthshire and Brecon Canal. Follow the track for just under 1½ miles; it is lined most of the way with attractive willows and silver birches and there are more fine views of Blorenge and the Usk Valley. On reaching Llanfoist Crossing, pass through a wooden barrier and turn left C beneath the Heads of the Valleys Road to retrace part of the outward route to the Usk Bridge on the edge of Abergavenny.

Cross the bridge and for the final section you can either continue along the outward route by taking the paved path beside the river, or alternatively head diagonally across the meadows, along a clear path that ducks into trees, close to some houses. Follow this to a kissing-gate in the far corner and continue through the Byfield Road car park to the road, where you turn right to return to the castle. ●

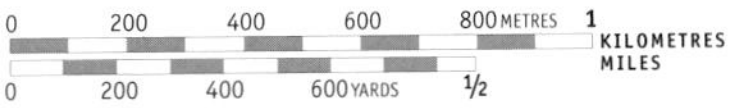

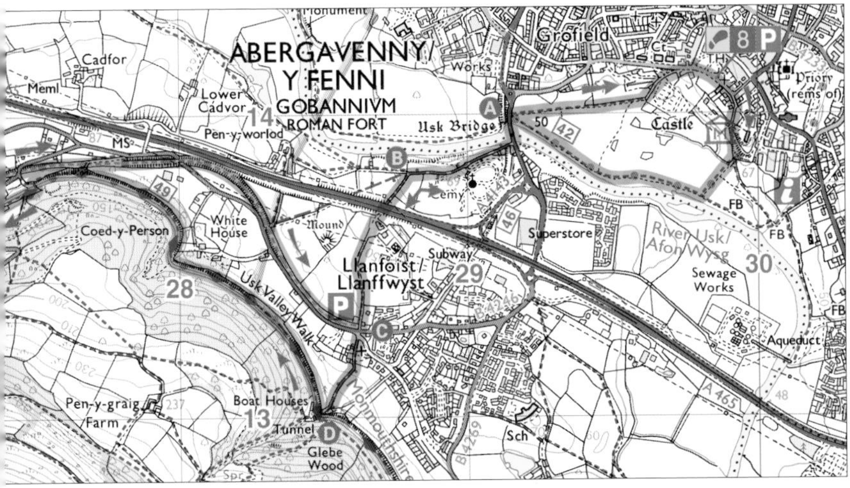

SCALE 1:25000 or 2½ INCHES to 1 MILE 4CM to 1KM

Mynydd Llangorse

Start	Cockit Hill
Distance	5½ miles (8.9km)
Height gain	1,115 feet (340m)
Approximate time	3 hours
Parking	Small parking area on bend at highest point of minor road 1¾ miles (2.8km) east of Llangors village
Route terrain	Clear paths and tracks around and across a high mountain. Some muddy stretches
Ordnance Survey maps	Landranger 161 (The Black Mountains), Explorer OL13 (Brecon Beacons National Park – Eastern area)

GPS waypoints

Start	SO 160 283
A	SO 168 266
B	SO 165 261
C	SO 159 250
D	SO 152 265

This circuit of Mynydd Llangorse provides superb and ever-changing views for remarkably little effort. The only strenuous section is the steep climb between Ⓐ *and* Ⓑ *out of the valley of Cwm Sorgwm on to the moorland plateau. The walk along the western slopes is particularly enjoyable.*

First head southwards down the lane and after a few yards bear right onto a track which keeps parallel to the lane but later bears gradually right away from it. Follow the track along the side of Cwm Sorgwm and below the eastern slopes of Mynydd Llangorse for about 1¼ miles. About 100 yds before reaching a metal gate, bear right Ⓐ onto a grassy path which heads up the hillside, clips a fence corner and then continues more steeply uphill.

Follow the path all the way up to a sharp right-hand bend and go around this before climbing a little more on to the plateau above. Now continue along a grassy path through bracken and heather to a prominent cairn Ⓑ. The only strenuous part of the walk is now over and from the cairn there are superb views over the Black Mountains and the Usk Valley.

Continue past the cairn over the open, breezy moorland on top of Mynydd Llangorse. Stay on the main path all the while, keeping right at one fork, and then left at second, to reach a crossroads of paths and tracks just in front of a small group of stunted trees, a rarity on this windswept plateau. Here turn left onto a broad grassy track and follow it past a boundary stone on the right after a few paces. Continue across open moorland, gradually curving left and heading gently downhill to a crossroads marked by a cairn Ⓒ. Turn right and follow the clear track, which runs parallel to a fence on the left and where it ends continue ahead. The path curves to the right to contour along the western slopes of Mynydd Llangorse. Descend to go through a gate, continue, passing to the right of a cottage and on across a meadow, before descending again through conifer woodland. Bear right, go through a gate and continue

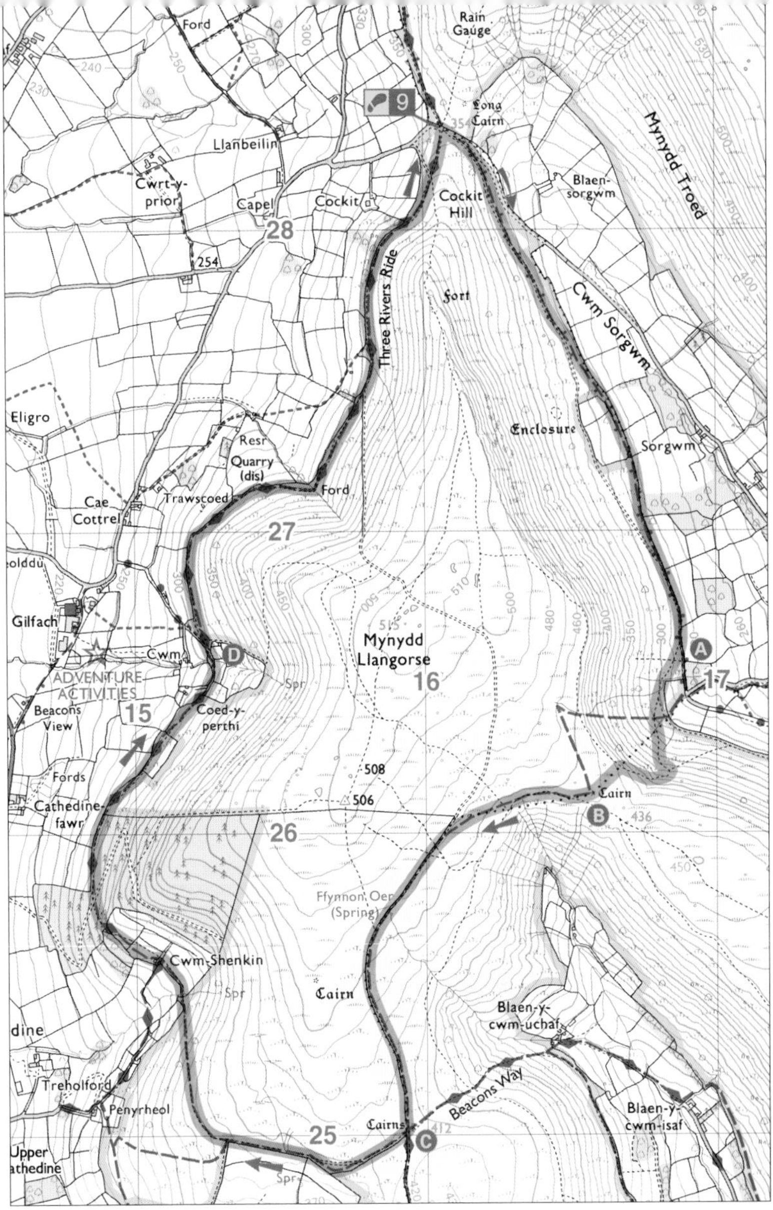

SCALE 1:25 000 or 2½ INCHES to 1 MILE 4CM to 1KM

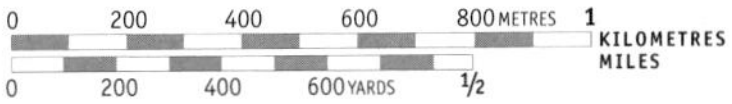

down through the wood. Cross a track and keep ahead along an attractive tree-lined path, by the bottom edge of woodland and with a wire fence on the left.

Go through a gate to leave the wood and continue, keeping by a fence on the left for almost the remainder of the walk. The western slopes of Mynydd Llangorse are more wooded than those on the eastern side and this part of the walk makes a striking contrast with the early section.

Ford a stream D and continue, taking the right-hand, upper path at the fork just in front. Continue along the same line, with a fence to your left and open hillside to the right, and cross another stream, now with the distinctive bulk of Mynydd Troed ahead. Eventually the path veers slightly right away from the fence and then leads back to the start. ●

Table Mountain

Start	Crickhowell
Distance	5 miles (8km)
Height gain	1,250 feet (380m)
Approximate time	3 hours
Parking	Pay and Display in Crickhowell
Route terrain	Easy paths over sheep pasture mixed with rougher mountain paths. Some steep climbs
Ordnance Survey maps	Landranger 161 (The Black Mountains), Explorer OL13 (Brecon Beacons National Park – Eastern area)

GPS waypoints

Start	SO 218 183
A	SO 221 183
B	SO 223 192
C	SO 227 205
D	SO 225 207
E	SO 218 208
F	SO 215 189

It is easy to see how Crug Hywel, with its distinctive flat top, lying just north of Crickhowell, gets its nickname of Table Mountain. From Crickhowell the 1,481-ft (451m) summit – crowned by an Iron Age fort and with a superb viewpoint – is reached via lanes, farm tracks and field and moorland paths. Both ascent and descent are gradual and relatively easy.

Crickhowell, with its many Georgian houses, gets its name from the mountain Crug Hywel. Crickhowell's most famous son is the surveyor Sir George Everest, after whom Mount Everest is named.

Begin in the main car park, off Greenhill Road. Walk back out onto Greenhill Road and turn left to walk uphill to a mini roundabout, where you turn right. Take the next left, Great Oak Road **A**, which is signed to Grwyne Fechan, and follow this road uphill for just over ½ mile, heading for Table Mountain in front. Where the road bends slightly right turn left through a metal gate **B**, at a public footpath sign, and take a tarmac track towards a farm.

Go through a metal gate, continue through the farmyard and in front of the farmhouse turn right through another metal gate. Keep straight ahead, with a hedge to your left, to a stile that leads onto an enclosed hedge-lined track. Turn left onto this and walk uphill to a stile. Climb it, continue along the right-hand edge of a field, climb another stile and head steadily uphill along the right-hand edge of the next field, by a wire fence and line of trees on the right, to climb a set of steps and another stile. Turn left onto a tarmac drive and leave it almost immediately to the right to climb a stile and continue along the right-hand edge of the next field, by a hedge on the right.

Climb a stile in the top corner and turn right to follow both the yellow waymark and a 'To the Mountain' sign along a pleasant, tree-lined path, passing to the left of a farmhouse. The next stile admits you to the open moorland of Table Mountain. Keep straight ahead to follow a clear, grassy path gently uphill between bracken over the lower slopes of the mountain, with a wall down to the right curving slightly left to a fork C. Here bear left along the upper path to continue contouring along the side of the mountain, and at the highest point on the shoulder take the path to the left for a brief detour to the summit. Pass through the rocks that mark the ramparts of the Iron Age fort to reach the summit cairn D, where there is a tremendous all-round view.

Continue to the highest point of the table, and follow a clear but steep path down beneath a rocky outcrop to level ground below. Keep ahead to meet the main path at a crossroads, and turn left, to drop slightly to a wall. Now follow the wall rightwards, following a path that meanders across the moorland, crossing several small streams and heading downhill. Pass a waymark post by a tumbledown building and continue, soon dropping steeply to a sheepfold in a corner. Enter this and turn left, as signposted, to a gate E.

Now continue down a walled track for a few paces, where you come to a short awkward section of about 20 yds along the bed of a stream – there are plenty of rocks to step on to keep your feet dry. Eventually the path spills into a narrow field, where you should keep ahead, with the stream now to your left, to woodland at the bottom. On the edge of the trees turn left to ford the stream and turn right through a metal gate to follow a sunken path downhill along the left-hand edge of the narrow, steep-sided, wooded valley of Cwm Cumbeth to a gate. Go through and continue along the edge of this delightful wooded valley, passing through a gate before coming to a fork with a new metal gate on the left, and a wooden stile to the right. Cross the wooden stile, which is signed Beacons Way, and follow the path straight down with the fence to your right, through a couple of fields and into a compound to the right of a barn.

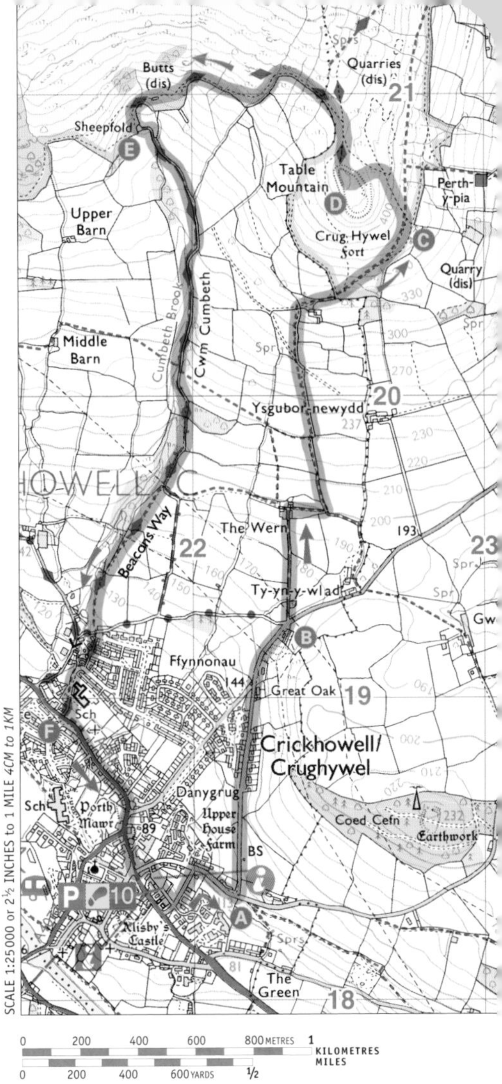

Cross the stile to the left of the stable buildings, and turn left onto a lane, and then immediately right, though a gate, onto a housing road. Walk straight across this to follow a tarmac footpath downhill between houses and cross another road, to follow another tarmac footpath to a junction with a third road. Turn right onto this and swing left to walk past a school. Where the road ends, keep ahead on a narrow pathway that leads down to the main road F. Turn left and walk past the **Bear Hotel** before bearing left up Standard Street and then right, back into the car park. ●

Craig y Cilau and Llangattock

		GPS waypoints
Start	Craig y Cilau	SO 185 168
Distance	5½ miles (8.8km). Shorter version 4½ miles (7.2km)	Ⓐ SO 187 174
Height gain	1,115 feet (340m). Shorter version 1,015 feet (310m)	Ⓑ SO 206 172 Ⓒ SO 207 177
Approximate time	3 hours (2½ hours for shorter versions)	Ⓓ SO 210 177 Ⓔ SO 207 171 Ⓕ SO 205 169
Parking	On verge below Craig y Cilau	Ⓖ SO 200 159
Route terrain	Clear paths and tracks around and across a high mountain. Some muddy stretches	
Ordnance Survey maps	Landranger 161 (The Black Mountains), Explorer OL13 (Brecon Beacons National Park – Eastern area)	

Craig y Cilau forms part of the northern edge of Mynydd Llangatwg, a steep, dramatic limestone escarpment overlooking the Usk Valley. Not only is it a fine viewpoint but it is of considerable botanical, geological and historic interest. The walk starts just below the escarpment and the first part of it is along field paths and quiet lanes, mostly through or along the edge of woodland, and includes a short but very attractive section along the towpath of the Monmouthshire and Brecon Canal and a visit to the village of Llangattock. Later there is a steep climb onto the escarpment, followed by a splendid walk across the face of it before the descent to return to the starting point. The shorter version of the walk omits the village of Llangattock.

Face uphill from the cattle-grid and look down to your right to find a waymarked stile. Climb this and keep close to the line of trees on your right, go through a metal gate in the bottom right-hand corner and follow a stony path into woodland. Keep straight ahead to drop to the bottom of the wood, and after emerging into a field bear left to keep parallel to its left-hand edge, which is bordered by woodland, descending steeply to the valley floor.

At the bottom, just before reaching a ford, turn right Ⓐ along a track which climbs gently above the wooded valley on the left. Where the track peters out keep ahead along the left-hand edge of a succession of fields, by the woodland of Coed y Cilau on the left, climbing a series of stiles. Eventually go through a metal gate, continue along an enclosed track, and after passing through another metal gate the track curves first to the right and then to the left to Cilau Farm.

At the boundary of the farm complex turn right at a fingerpost and climb the waymarked stile at the corner. Walk the field edge behind the barns and farmhouse to a stile onto a tarred lane. Turn left and then take the stile on the right at the corner, keeping along the left edge of the subsequent field. Climb another stile, bear half right across the next field, making for a stile and public footpath sign on its right-hand edge, and climb the stile onto a lane. Turn left, cross the canal bridge **B** and turn right down to the canal.

For the shorter version of the walk, omitting Llangattock, turn left here and walk along the towpath to the next bridge about 100 yds ahead. Pass under it and turn left up to a lane, turning left to rejoin the full walk at **E**.

Turn right under the bridge and then continue along the right bank of the canal for nearly ½ mile, as far as the next bridge. This is a delightful stretch of the Monmouthshire and Brecon Canal: it is tree-lined, tranquil and with some lovely views through gaps in trees on the right of Llangattock church, the Usk Valley, Crickhowell and on the horizon the distinctive, flat top of Table Mountain.

At the bridge **C** turn right through a gateway, and turn right downhill along a lane, following it around a right-hand bend into Llangattock, an attractive village of narrow streets, old cottages and a solid-looking medieval church. The lane passes a new housing development all the way up to a sharp right-hand bend and go around this

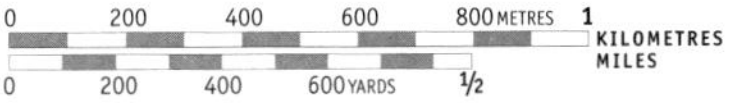

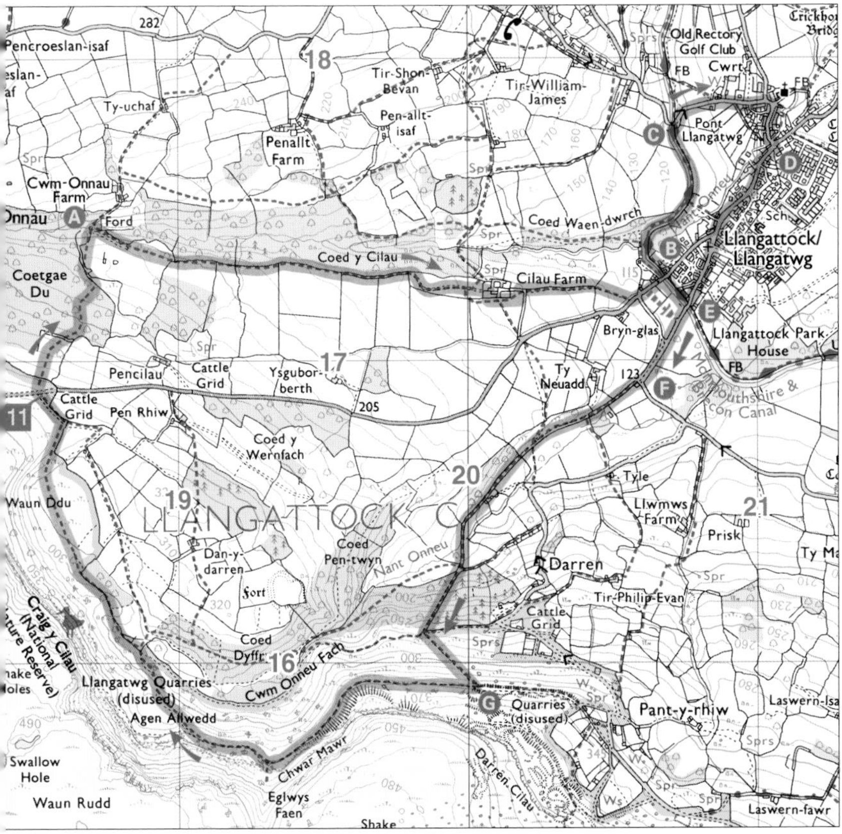

SCALE 1:25 000 or 2½ INCHES to 1 MILE *4CM to 1KM*

Craig y Cilau

before climbing a little more on to the plateau above. Now go through the village to a T-junction **D**. Turn right along the road signposted to Beaufort and keep straight ahead at a fork, by a chapel on the right. Cross a canal bridge **E** and continue along the lane for another 1/4 mile. In front looms the forbidding-looking escarpment of Craig y Cilau.

Where the lane bends left turn right **F** over a stile, at a public footpath sign, almost immediately following the direction of another public footpath sign to the left. Walk along a grassy path, by a hedge on the left; this was once part of a tramway that carried stone from the quarries on Mynydd Llangatwg to Llangattock Wharf on the Monmouthshire and Brecon Canal. The path later becomes enclosed and continues through woodland. Go through a metal gate, keep ahead to go through another and continue along this attractive, partially tree-lined path. Soon after passing to the right of a cottage the path bears left to cross a stream and continues along the right-hand edge of a field to a stile at the foot of a steep incline. This incline was the means by which wagons loaded with limestone were lowered down the escarpment into the valley from where they were carried via the tramway to the canal.

Climb the stile and then climb the incline, which is in two parts. This is by far the most strenuous and tiring part of the walk. On reaching a flatter open area at the top of the first incline keep ahead for a few yards and then turn left to climb a second incline, slightly less steep and stony than the first one, turning sharp right at the top onto a track **G**. Now comes the most scenic and one of the easiest parts of the walk along this broad, flat, well-surfaced track, also a former quarry tramway, as it contours across the face of the escarpment, with magnificent views to the right over the Usk Valley, Crickhowell, Table Mountain and the Black Mountains, and a spectacular view in front of the line of the curving escarpment. A notice says that you are entering Craig y Cilau National Nature Reserve, noted for its cave systems, rare flora and limestone woodland.

The old trackbed passes below the entrance to Eglwys Faen cave and then curves beneath an old quarry face. At the far end of this look carefully for a waymark post indicating a path forking off to the right. Take this, which descends gradually across the steep slope. In 200 yds you will reach a waymarked split in the path. Keep right dropping through woodland of gnarled hawthorns to reach a wood. Keep this on your right; the path undulates through tumbled boulders and beneath contorted old ash trees to gain an open area of common.

Head diagonally across this, passing just to the right of two fenced areas and aiming for an obvious path up the hillside ahead. Pass by another Nature Reserve sign and trace the fence through to a rough lane. Turn left onto this to return to the cattle-grid and the starting point of the walk. ●

Tor y Foel

Start	Llangynidr
Distance	5½ miles (8.9km)
Height gain	1,575 feet (480m)
Approximate time	3 hours
Parking	Small free parking area at Lower Lock
Route terrain	Mainly easy to follow, waymarked paths and tracks over farmland and open hilltops
Ordnance Survey maps	Landranger 161 (The Black Mountains), Explorer OL13 (Brecon Beacons National Park – Eastern area)

GPS waypoints

Start	SO 146 200
A	SO 144 197
B	SO 134 193
C	SO 114 194
D	SO 113 204
E	SO 127 200

The lonely outlier of Tor y Foel is wedged between the central Brecon Beacons and the Black Mountains, and although it offers fine views over both massifs, it actually belongs to neither. It's one of those mountains that can be seen from just about anywhere; and its distinctive lofty, yet rounded outline is easily recognised, no matter where it's viewed. The hill is at its most impressive from the Usk Valley, where the steep north and west flanks really do look quite daunting. Yet it's not difficult to climb, especially from the east, where good, well-waymarked paths lead through a succession of sheep pastures all the way to the summit. This walk makes the most of these paths to tackle the peak from east to west. It returns on scenic paths that drop easily into the Usk Valley, finishing on a delightful stretch of the Monmouthshire & Brecon Canal.

The walk starts at Llangynidr's Lower Lock, which is one of five locks in the Llangynidr area. There's parking here for a few cars. Follow the towpath away from the lock with the canal to your left and walk beneath the bridge carrying the B4558. Now round a long right-hand bend and when you reach the first of the next locks

Tor y Foel from Table Mountain

Ⓐ, bear left, over the little bridge, to follow a clear footpath up through woodland to a stile, which is waymarked with a Beacons Way disk. Continue through the woodland to another stile which leads out onto open pasture, and keep straight ahead across the field to another stile, still following the Beacons Way. Bear right to follow the hedge to another stile and cross this and turn left to follow the field edge up to a drive.

Go straight across this and continue in the same direction, towards the top corner, where you need to cross another stile. Now continue in the same direction, all the time following Beacons Way signs, until you reach a lane ahead of a farmhouse. Turn right onto this and follow it up and around to the left, where you need to turn right onto a tree-lined track Ⓑ.

Now follow this straight up, keeping to the right-hand edge of the field the whole time, with great views ahead to Tor y Foel. Continue like this until a stile ahead leads into a narrow finger of open hillside, with a plantation to your right. Now continue straight ahead, passing the end of the plantation and climbing steeply up onto the summit

SCALE 1:25 000 or 2½ INCHES to 1 MILE *4CM to 1KM*

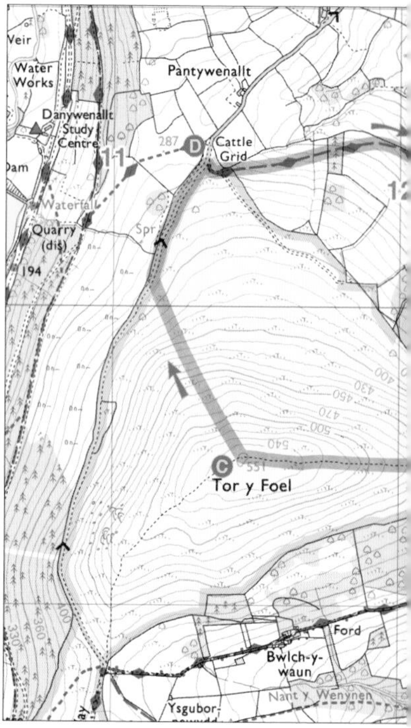

Waun Rhycl and the Talybont Reservoir from Tor y Foel

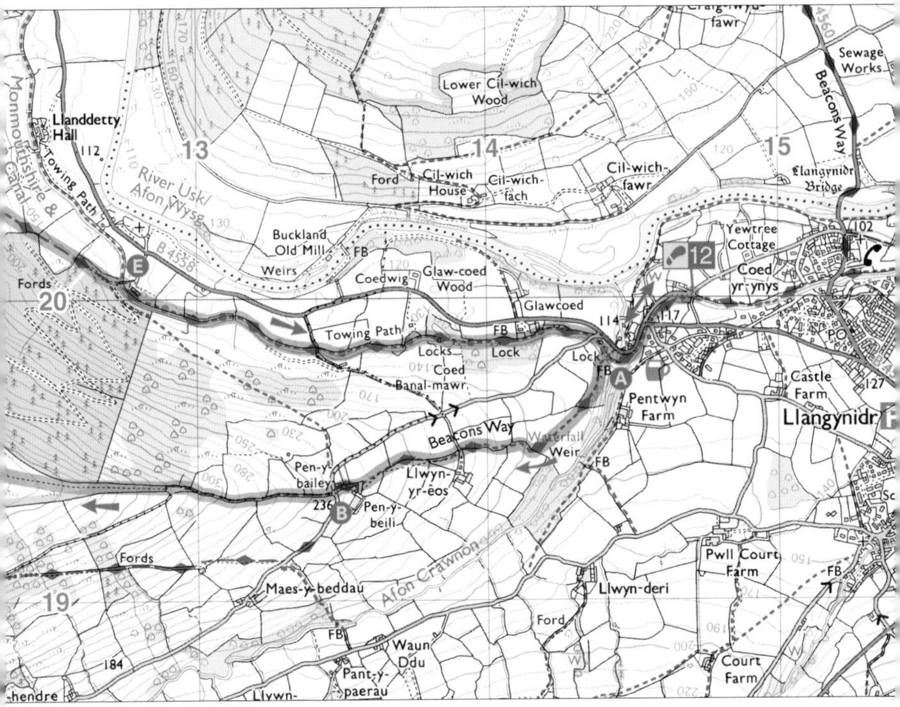

C. The very top is marked by the smallest of cairns but the views are absolutely magnificent with the Talybont Forest and Reservoir stretched out at your feet and the imposing bulk of the main Brecon Beacons dominating the vista directly ahead. There are also fine views down to the south, to the Crawnon Valley – a rarely visited glen that slices decisively into the limestone wastes of Mynydd Llangynidr.

To descend, turn right, away from the main path onto a narrower, fainter path that descends towards the north west. Follow this easily down to the narrow road below and turn right onto this to follow it downhill for 500 yds to an obvious, broad muddy track on the right. Take this, and climb uphill slightly, before curving left and dropping to a gate D. Now follow the path across the hillside towards the middle of a band of trees ahead. Go through a gate and continue across another field, dropping all the time until

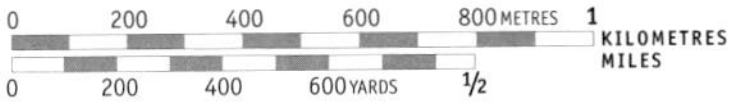

you have the hedge to your left. Now continue through another gate and along the bottom edge of another field to yet another gate. Carry on in the same direction, dropping all the time, and cross a stream before going though another gate at the bottom corner of a wood. Keep heading in the same direction, passing through further gates until you eventually reach a hedged track that leads easily down to a bridge over the Monmouthshire & Brecon Canal E. Cross the bridge and turn right onto the towpath to walk easily along with the canal to your right.

You'll soon reach the first of three locks in quick succession, and after another few minutes, you'll reach a boatyard and another lock, where you crossed the canal earlier. Keep straight ahead to curve back round beneath the B4558 and continue back to the start. ●

Ystradfellte and Sarn Helen

Start	Ystradfellte
Distance	6½ miles (10.4km)
Height gain	2,100 feet (640m)
Approximate time	3½ hours
Parking	Free car park in Ystradfellte
Route terrain	Mainly good paths and tracks with a short section on a very quiet lane. *One section of moor would require careful navigation in poor visibility*
Ordnance Survey maps	Landranger 160 (Brecon Beacons), Explorer OL12 (Brecon Beacons National Park – Western area)

GPS waypoints

- Start SN 929 134
- A SN 924 138
- B SN 926 154
- C SN 925 166
- D SN 911 148
- E SN 907 138
- F SN 912 141

This is a surprisingly tough walk through an austere, atmospheric limestone landscape with wonderful views over the empty expanses of the Fforest Fawr mountain range. The highlights include a lovely section of Sarn Helen – an old Roman road that runs almost the full length of Wales – and the impressive standing stone of Maen Madoc, resplendent with a Roman inscription.

The isolated hamlet of Ystradfellte comprises little more than a church, a pub, a post office and a few houses, but it makes an excellent walking centre.

Start: Go through a gap at the top of the car park and turn left onto a tarmac track that leads uphill through a metal gate. Where the tarmac track turns right to Tyle Farm continue uphill along an enclosed track, passing through two metal gates to emerge onto open moorland A.

Ignoring a public footpath sign to the left, keep ahead, by a wall on the right, along a grassy path which heads straight across an austere, open landscape of grass, heather and isolated trees, littered with limestone boulders. Go through a metal gate and continue between the crags of Carnau Gwynion to another metal gate. Go through that to walk along a wide, walled, grassy track from which there are superb views ahead over mountains, moorland and forest. Go through a gate and follow the track to a road B. Keep ahead along the road for 3/4 mile, entering conifer plantations and passing Blaen Llia car park.

Just after the car park entrance there is a grand view ahead up the valley and to the right across the bare slopes of Fan Dringarth. About 1/4 mile past the car park turn sharp left C onto a broad track (waymarked Sarn Helen), go through a metal gate and follow the track through conifers. This track follows a well-preserved stretch of Sarn Helen, a Roman road that linked South and North Wales. Here it runs across the open moorlands of Fforest Fawr between the forts of Nidum (Neath) and Y Gaer, near Brecon. After going through another metal gate, leave the trees and continue across open moorland, with fine sweeping views across the valley of the River Neath, passing the isolated standing stone of Maen Madoc. It is probably of Celtic origin but the Romans later carved a Latin inscription on it. The track winds downhill, bending right through a metal gate to reach a bridge that spans the Afon Nedd Fechan **D**.

Cross the bridge and continue along Sarn Helen, at first climbing steeply on a very rough surface. Continue all the way up to a gate at the corner of a plantation. Go through and bear half

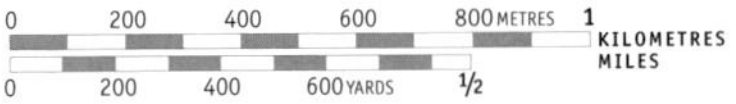

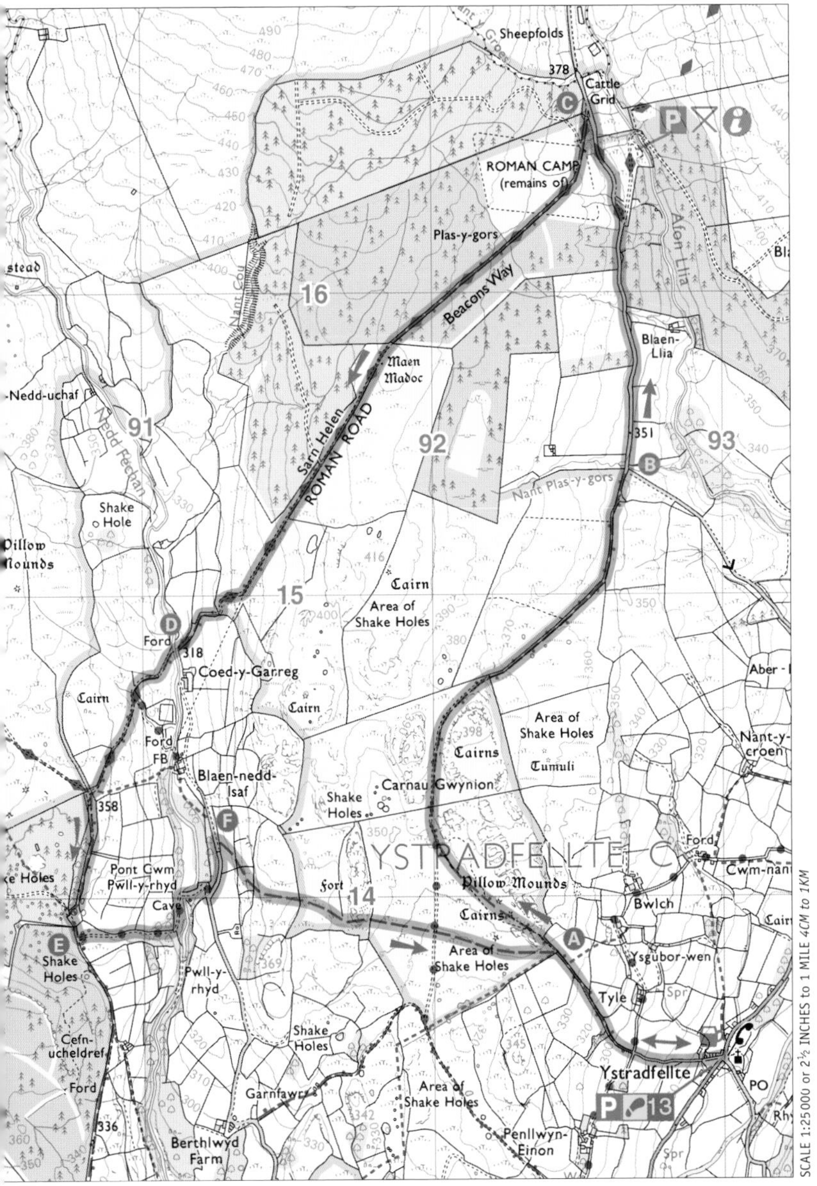

The isolated standing stone of Maen Madoc

left onto a good track that's signed Sarn Helen, and follow this with the wood to your right past a turning that comes in from the right to another gate by a large shake hole. Go through this and after a few more paces, turn left onto a clear track that heads downhill Ⓔ.

Follow this steeply downhill and around to the left and then right to cross an old bridge over the Afon Nedd Fechan. Climb steeply away from the bridge and at the top, turn left onto a lane. Follow this for a few paces to a gate and a footpath sign to Ystradfellte Ⓕ. Go through and turn sharp right to head diagonally uphill across a field to go through a gate in the top corner and continue in the same direction across the next field and through the trees to another gate. Continue once more across open grassy moorland, passing a waymark post and passing through two more gates; the second close to the brow of a hill. Pass to the right of the remains of an Iron Age fort and go through another gate. Now keep straight ahead across the moorland – there is no obvious path – heading downhill and making for a circular fence in front enclosing a shake hole – a depression in the limestone – one of many in this area.

Cross a track, pass to the left of the circular fence and bear slightly left – again there is no obvious path – aiming to the top of the hill, from where you should be able to make out the wall corner Ⓐ. Here bear right through a metal gate and retrace your steps downhill to Ystradfellte. ●

The Blorenge

Start	Keeper's Pond (Pen-ffordd-goch Pond)
Distance	6 miles (9.8km)
Height gain	1,250 feet (380m)
Approximate time	3 hours
Parking	Keeper's Pond free car park, just off the B4246, halfway between Llanfoist and Blaenavon
Route terrain	Mainly clear paths and tracks over rough mountain-side. *One steep descent and one short, steep climb*
Ordnance Survey maps	Landranger 161 (The Black Mountains), Explorer OL13 (Brecon Beacons National Park – Eastern area)

GPS waypoints

Start	SO 254 107
A	SO 264 119
B	SO 269 127
C	SO 282 116
D	SO 278 112
E	SO 277 122
F	SO 263 107

The formidable bulk of the Blorenge towers high above Abergavenny and the Usk Valley and is unique in being the only peak of any significance in the National Park that actually sits south of the A465 Heads of the Valleys road. It's famous not just for the magnificent views but also for some fascinating industrial history, standing as it does, above the small town of Blaenavon, famous for both iron and coal production. The surrounding area also features in the classic Rape of the Fair Country *novel by Alexander Cordell. An inn bearing his name is just down the hill from the start and finish.*

Keepers pond was once used to feed steam engines at the Garnddyrys Forge, about 3/4 mile on the hillside below. It got its name from the gamekeeper's cottage that was once situated nearby.

(Start) From the car park, walk down to the pond and turn left, keep it to your right. Now follow the clear path around the southern tip, where you'll find a well-surfaced, wheelchair-friendly path that carries on along the western shore, keeping the pond to the right the whole time. Continue to the very far end and cross a footbridge before bearing slightly right to continue on a clear grassy path that runs easily along with the main ridge up to the right.

This gradually veers around to the right to reveal great views over the Usk Valley and the town of Abergavenny. Stay with it, passing through a shallow, stony cutting at one stage, until you reach a junction marked with a small post (A). Turn left here, signed to Llanfoist and Govilon, and follow it steeply down for a few paces until the gradient eases slightly and it bears around to the right again to continue around the hillside, dropping slightly as it goes. It ends at a junction with a broader, clearer track above a wood (B). Turn right onto this, which is actually the line of an old tram road known as Hill's Tram Road after the local Iron

Master, Thomas Hill, and follow it easily around the hillside, ignoring a footpath that drops down to the left. Pass a tunnel to your right and stay with the track, which continues to contour around the hillside, until you eventually reach a gate that leads into the Punchbowl Nature Reserve.

Keep straight ahead again and soon you'll come to the lovely pond at the heart of the Punchbowl C. Keep the water to your right and keep straight ahead to climb steeply on a rough track that leads beneath towering beech trees before levelling slightly at a gate. Go through this and continue to another gate alongside a plantation. Keep ahead again and another gate leads out onto a narrow lane.

Turn right onto the lane, and after passing the end of the plantation on the right, turn right again onto a narrow path, waymarked to the Blorenge D. Follow this upwards, with the wall to your right, and continue to a small marker post where the wall veers right, away from the path. Keep straight ahead climbing steadily upwards and keeping right when you join another path that comes in from the left. Stay with this all the way to the top, where it passes through some small grassy humps, once piles of quarry spoil, and levels out, with wonderful views to the right.

Continue until you reach a small brick hut E and here turn left to climb steeply up a peaty and stony path that soon levels again. Now stay with this main path all the way to the summit, which is marked with a trig point concealed in the rocks. To descend, keep ahead to follow a continuation path towards the two huge masts that you can see in the distance. As you get close to the masts and the car park beneath them, look for a faint path to the right that leads to a seat. Cross the bank

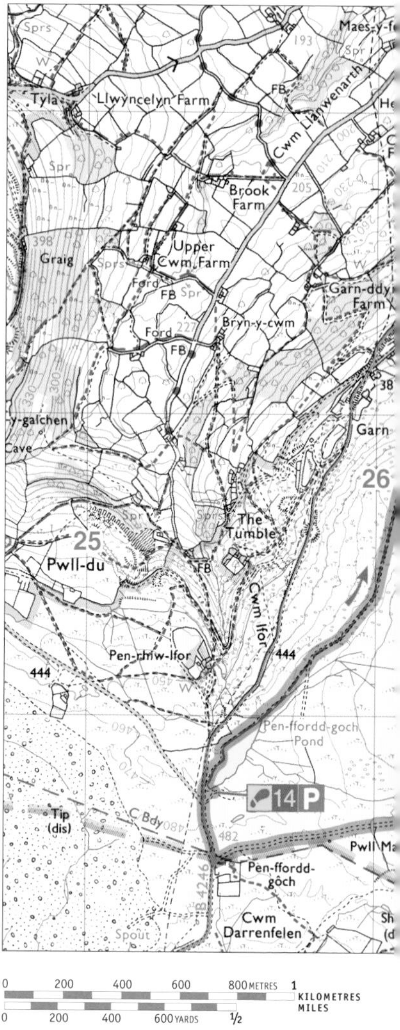

behind the seat and you'll find a plaque that marks the spot of Foxhunter's Grave.

Foxhunter was a champion show jumper that won Britain's only gold medal in the 1952 Olympic Games, in Helsinki, ridden by Welshman, Sir Harry Llewellyn. Together they won nearly 80 international trophies until Foxhunter died in 1959. He was buried at this spot, high on the Blorenge and Sir Harry's ashes were scattered there with him some 40 years later.

Turn left onto the path here and

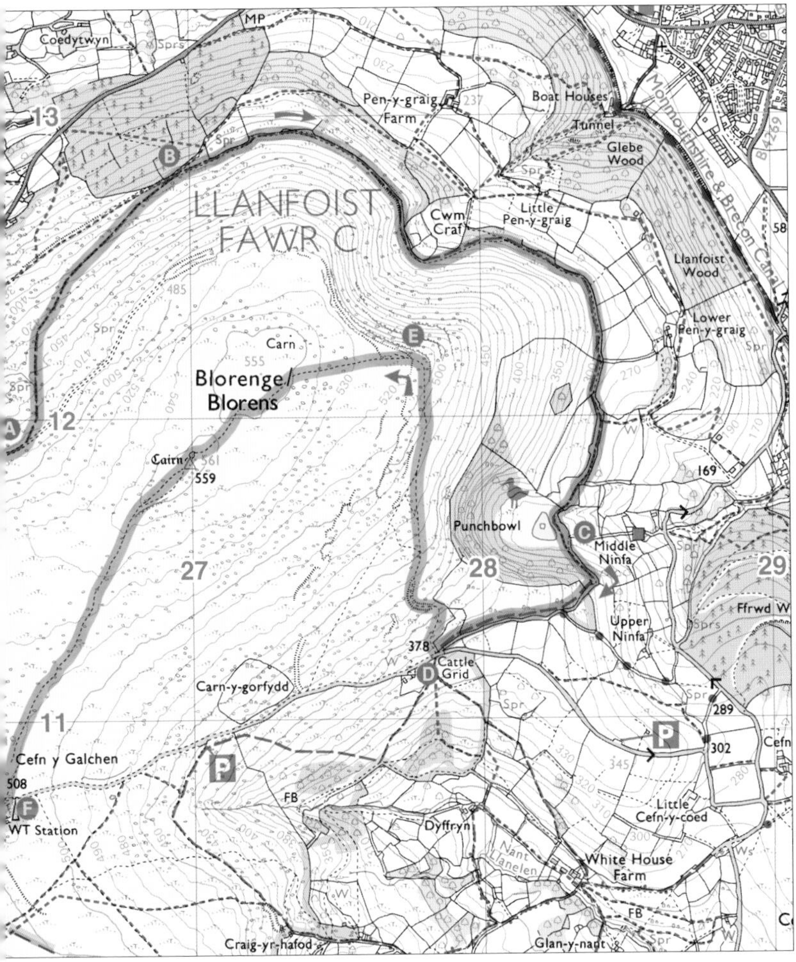

SCALE 1:25 000 or 2½ INCHES to 1 MILE *4CM to 1KM*

follow it easily to the car park F. Carry on out onto the road and turn right to follow this all the way down to a junction with the B4246. Turn right onto this and then right again to return to Keeper's Pond. ●

Keeper's Pond

Fan Fawr

Start	Storey Arms Centre
Distance	4½ miles (7.3km)
Height gain	1,325 feet (405m)
Approximate time	3 hours
Parking	Free parking opposite the Storey Arms on the A470 between Brecon and Merthyr Tydfil
Route terrain	Mainly faint and rough paths across moorland and high mountains. Some boggy sections
Ordnance Survey maps	Landranger 160 (Brecon Beacons), Explorer OL12 (Brecon Beacons National Park – Western area)

GPS waypoints

- SN 982 203
- Ⓐ SN 987 195
- Ⓑ SN 984 184
- Ⓒ SN 988 180
- Ⓓ SN 969 193

The contrast between the mountains of Fforest Fawr and the central Brecon Beacons could not be more marked. While hundreds of walkers ascend the summits of Corn Du and Pen y Fan every day, far fewer turn their sights west, to the steep grassy slopes of Fan Fawr. This walk, a short but quite strenuous ramble, scales this peak ascending its shapely and easy-angled south-east ridge. Like most of the Fforest Fawr massif, the paths are faint and the ground is boggy in places, so it's best not tackled in poor visibility.

The Storey Arms was once a coaching inn, ideally placed at the top of the pass that would have carried most of the traffic through the mountains in those days. Today the building is an adventure centre, surrounded by busy car parks that make ideal starting places for walks to the highest mountains in the National Park.

Summit Cairn, Fan Fawr

From the higher of the two car parks, opposite the Storey Arms, cross the road and walk along the opposite verge until you can fork slightly left to walk through the slip road that actually makes up the lower car park. Continue to the very bottom, where a stile leads into a conifer plantation. Follow the narrow path to another stile that leads back onto the verge and then cross the road to continue for a few paces on the other side. At a tall Taff Trail waymark, drop to the right to continue on a narrow path that runs beneath a bank. Stay with this to a waymarked kissing-gate Ⓐ that leads out onto open moorland next to the Afon Taf Fawr.

Cross a footbridge and follow a boggy path along the river bank to the edge of a wood, where you should turn right to climb steeply up to a clearer track that then follows the line of the wood leftwards. Stay with this, keeping the wood to the left the whole time and after dropping into a deep river gulley and climbing back out again, you'll come to a waymarked stile in the fence on the left Ⓑ. Cross this and turn almost immediately right onto a broad forest track that runs high above the Beacons Reservoir before dropping to the A4059 Ⓒ. Turn right, onto a verge, and follow the road uphill with the wood to the right for around 100 yds. Cross a cattle-grid and pass the end of the wood, then turn right onto a faint path that improves as it goes. Bear half

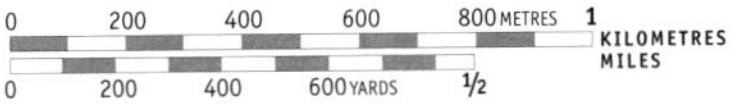

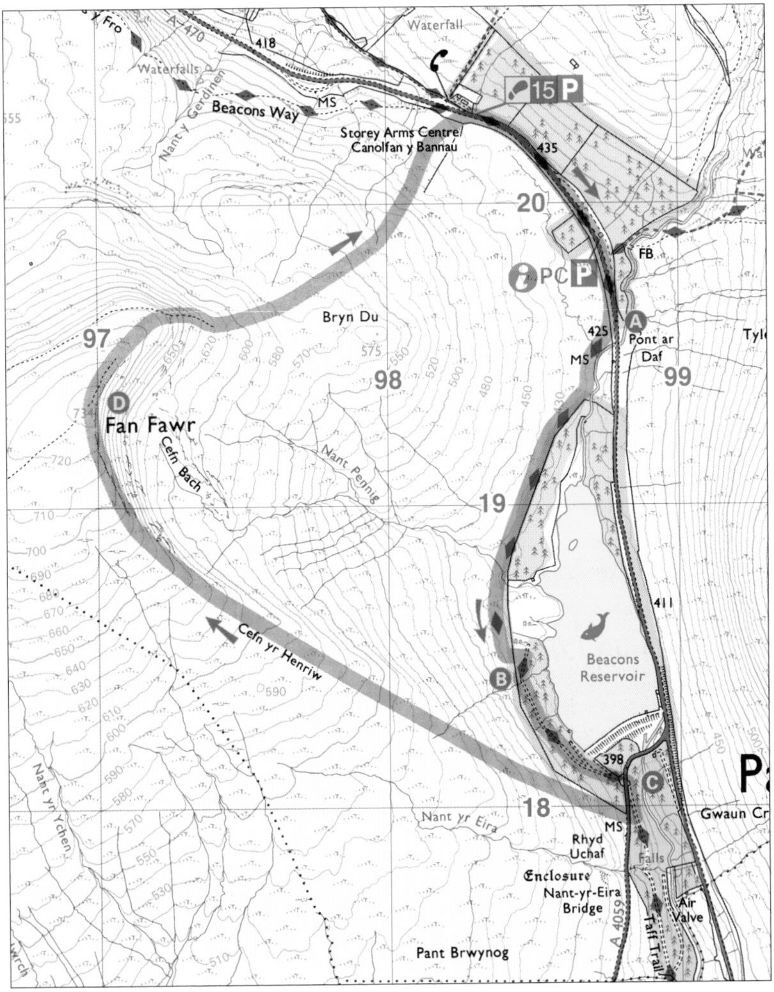

SCALE 1:25000 or 2½ INCHES to 1 MILE 4CM to 1KM

Fan Fawr from Pen y Fan

left to follow the path, all the way up onto the south-east ridge of Fan Fawr; with magnificent views ahead to the steep eastern escarpment. Continue to the very top, and trace your way around the escarpment edge to the true summit, which is marked with a diminutive cairn Ⓓ.

Although less-walked than Corn Du and Pen y Fan, which dominate the skyline on the other side of the valley, Fan Fawr offers equally spectacular views including, of course, a true high-level close-up of the highest peaks themselves. From the cairn, continue around the escarpment edge, with fantastic views into the valley below, and stay with the path as it starts to drop steeply down the eastern flanks of the mountain.

Eventually it levels and continues easily onto the boggy plateau of Bryn Du, where the path starts to become vague again. Keep ahead, aiming all the time for the left-hand side of the wood you can see opposite, on the flanks of Corn Du. After a few paces the car park comes into sight and you should be able to follow faint paths and sheep tracks all the way back down to the road. ●

Sugar Loaf

Start	Llangenny	**GPS waypoints**
Distance	6 miles (9.7km)	SO 239 181
Height gain	1,900 feet (580m)	Ⓐ SO 240 179
Approximate time	3½ hours	Ⓑ SO 244 194
Parking	Limited parking by the church or ask for permission at the Dragon's Head pub	Ⓒ SO 253 189 Ⓓ SO 272 187 Ⓔ SO 260 182 Ⓕ SO 243 178
Route terrain	Mainly clear paths and tracks over farmland and rough mountainside. Some steep sections	
Ordnance Survey maps	Landranger 161 (The Black Mountains), Explorer OL13 (Brecon Beacons National Park – Eastern area)	

The Sugar Loaf is one the most popular mountains in the Brecon Beacons National Park, and its distinctive conical summit can be seen from miles around, especially when approaching from the east. It's a wonderful viewpoint, all the better for being set back a little from the main Black Mountains massif, which it views from across the pretty valley of the Grwyne Fawr. This walk climbs to the summit from a small village on the floor of this scenic valley.

Walk back towards the main bridge, by the **Dragon's Head** pub, cross it, then turn left to climb over a stone stile in the wall on your left Ⓐ. Follow the path easily along the banks of the river into Pendarren Park, and keep ahead, following the well-signed footpath, until you reach a second footbridge, where you go through a gate and turn immediately right to follow a clear path up to join another clear grassy track that you turn left onto to follow around the hillside to a farm. Cross a stile into the yard, and keep slightly right to another stile, that leads onto a lane Ⓑ.

Turn right and walk along the road for 1/4 mile to a narrow lane on the left. Take this and walk up past a house on the right, and then, as you reach another farm, bear left onto a waymarked bridleway. Follow this around the hillside to a junction between two gates, and bear right to walk steeply uphill to another gate, which gives access to open hillside. Keep ahead, with the fence, then wall, on your right and aim for some rough ground at the foot of Sugar Loaf's obvious west ridge ahead Ⓒ. Keep ahead to follow a clear path up onto this ridge and stay with it to the crest where another path forks in from the right. Now follow the crest all the way up to the summit of the Sugar Loaf, with fine views over the mountain all the way.

Cross the summit ridge to the trig point Ⓓ, where you get splendid views over the Usk Valley to the Blorenge, as well as the Black Mountains to the west, and Ysgyryd Fawr to the east. You'll

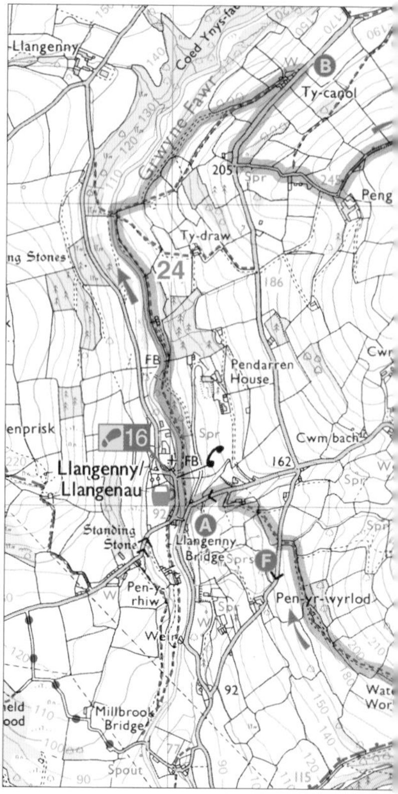

also see Abergavenny tucked beneath the foot of the mountain, and the distinctive gash of the Clydach Gorge heading uphill from the village of Gilwern, on the other side of the Usk. Now bear right to follow a clear path steeply down the face of the mountain. There are a few different paths dropping down, but if you keep to the right as much as possible, with a distinct valley between you and the ridge you've just climbed, you cannot go far wrong. As the ground levels, fork right, to drop through bracken to a stream in the valley bottom, by the corner of a coniferous wood Ⓔ.

Cross the stream and turn immediately left to walk down to a gate. Now keep ahead on a clear path that crosses sheep pastures. Eventually, bearing left onto a sheltered track, that drops to a junction with another track. Turn right onto this and follow it down past a lovely house to the road head. Turn right to climb steeply up to the waterworks and then bear left, over a stile, to follow a footpath straight across a field. Cross another stile and keep to the bottom of the next field to a stile on the left. Cross this and turn right to follow the field edge through a wooded area and past a ruined building. Now keep ahead and you'll follow a sunken track all the way out to another road Ⓕ.

Sugar loaf from Mynydd Llangatwg

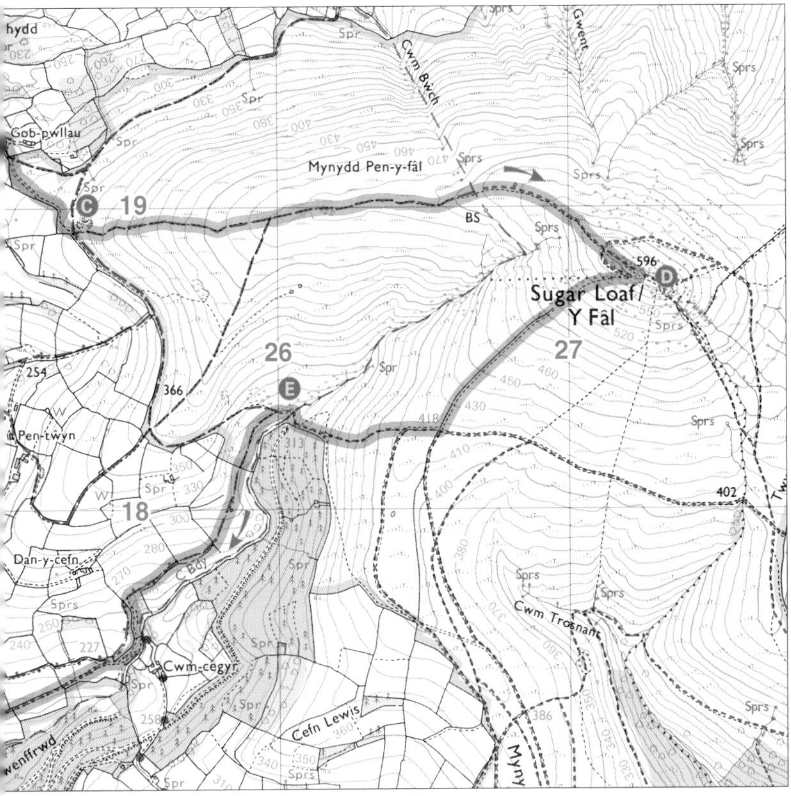

SCALE 1:25 000 or 2½ INCHES to 1 MILE *4CM to 1KM*

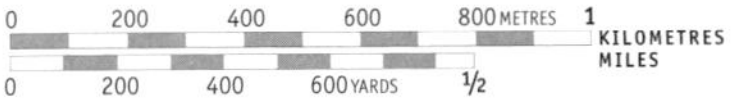

Cross this, and climb over the stile opposite. Now bear half-right to cross the next field and cross another stile to drop down beside a house. Bear right at the bottom, and follow the drive out to the road, where you should turn left to drop to the bridge where you started. ●

Cwm Oergwm

Start	Llanfrynach
Distance	7 miles (11.3km)
Height gain	1,020 feet (310m)
Approximate time	3½ hours
Parking	Street-side parking in Llanfrynach
Route terrain	Quiet lanes, wooded paths, rough paths over moorland. An awkward stream crossing that's best not tackled after extensive rain
Ordnance Survey maps	Landranger 160 (Brecon Beacons), Explorer OL12 (Brecon Beacons National Park – Western area)

GPS waypoints

- SO 074 257
- Ⓐ SO 075 257
- Ⓑ SO 064 239
- Ⓒ SO 058 228
- Ⓓ SO 047 214
- Ⓔ SO 047 216
- Ⓕ SO 049 220
- Ⓖ SO 057 233
- Ⓗ SO 057 240
- Ⓙ SO 065 249

The high mountains of the central Brecon Beacons are defined as much by the wonderful, steep-sided cwms that radiate from them, as by the summits themselves, and this walk delves deep into the eastern-most of these beautiful valleys: Cwm Oergwm, offering fine views of the towering peaks of Fan y Big and Cribyn, as well as visiting a delightful chain of small cascades on the Nant Menasgin.

With the toilets to your right and the church to your left, walk along the road for a few paces and turn right by the telephone box Ⓐ. Follow this across the bridge and then turn first right, up a narrow lane (Tregaer Road). Follow this hedged lane easily up into the valley, with the occasional tantalising glimpse of the high mountains ahead, and continue for just over 1 mile past the farm at Caerau and past another house, where tarmac gives way to a dirt track at a gate Ⓑ.

Continue for ¼ mile to a fork and go straight ahead, through a waymarked gate, into forest. Keep ahead for another ½ mile to ford a stream and go through a gate that leads out onto National Trust ground Ⓒ. Bear slightly right to follow a green track by a tumbledown wall and stay with this to another gate. Keep straight ahead again and you'll

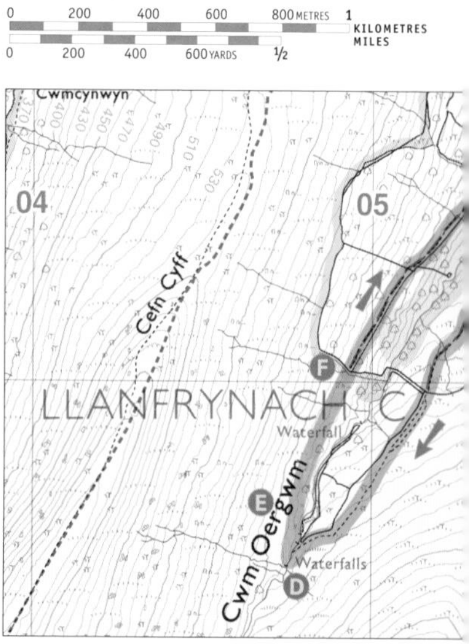

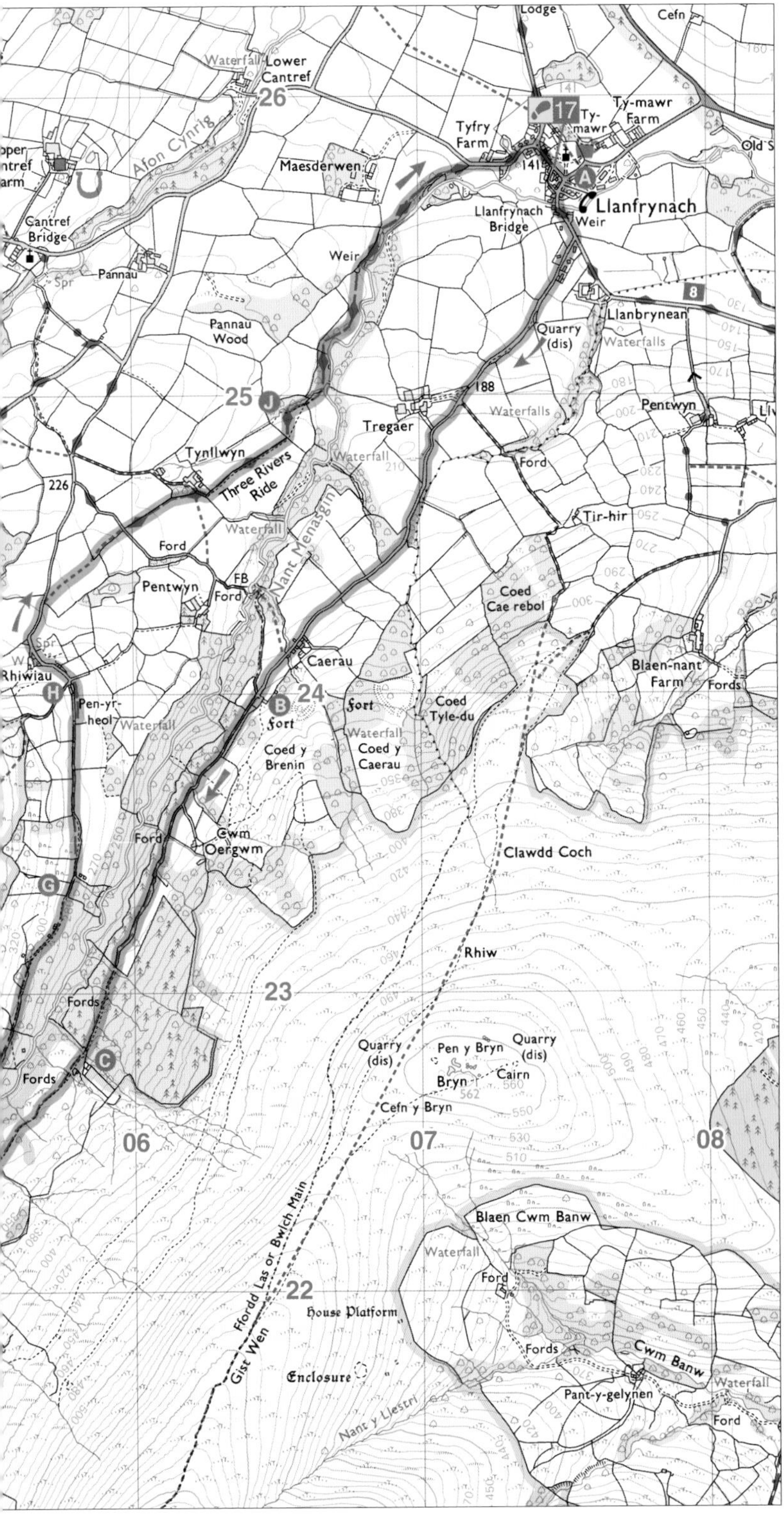

SCALE 1:25 000 or 2½ INCHES to 1 MILE *4CM to 1KM*

eventually come to another gate that leads out onto open moorland, with the peaks of Fan y Big and Cribyn towering above you at the head of the valley.

Continue on a rough path, with a tumbledown wall to your right, and when the path veers right to drop to the Nant Menasgin, bear right onto an obvious path to follow it, with a huge boulder to your left. Drop down to the stream and cross at the obvious ford **D**, where you'll see a lovely succession of waterfalls tumbling down the hillside above. If the stream is in spate, it may be easier to cross above the waterfalls, but if the levels are too high, it may be better to return the way you came.

Cascades on the Nant Menasgin, Cwm Oergym

A rough path leads away from the stream on the other bank. Follow this up for around 100 yds and keep your eyes peeled for a much fainter path forking off to the right **E**. Take this, and follow it around the hillside, neither climbing nor dropping.

This leads to a gate **F**, waymarked with a bridleway arrow, which you should go through to continue in the same direction. Keep ahead to another gate and then fork slightly left to follow waymarks uphill alongside a tumbledown wall. Ignore a fork to the left and continue to a metal farm gate. Do not go through this but instead head to the left of it and continue to a small bridlegate **G**.

Follow this up, where it becomes a sunken track and stay with this until, after a dark, tree-lined section, you see a gate ahead, blocking the obvious route. The bridleway has been diverted here so bear slightly right into the field, and then turn left to continue parallel to the original track, beneath some houses, to a waymarked gate just beyond **H**.

Turn right onto the lane, and then, after 300 yds, turn right, through a waymarked gate, onto a footpath. Take this diagonally left across the field to a stile in the corner, and then keep the hedge to your right to drop to a lane. Cross this and go through the gate ahead to continue straight down the left-hand edge of the field to another gate. Go through this and keep ahead to another, and then bear slightly left to drop to a series of waymark posts above a stream **J**.

Bear right as directed and continue to another post that sends you left, through a gate and over a brook. Now follow the obvious path ahead, with the Nant Menasgin to your right, and eventually break out into sheep pastures, where you continue with the stream and trees to your right in the same direction to a gate that leads onto a narrow lane. Turn right onto this and then turn right again to return to Llanfrynach. ●

Mynydd Illtud and Cefn Llechid

Start	Mynydd Illtud. Brecon Beacons Mountain Centre 1½ miles (2.4km) west of Libanus
Distance	7½ miles (12.1km)
Height gain	1,085 feet (330m)
Approximate time	4 hours
Parking	Brecon Beacons Mountain Centre at Mynydd Illtud (Pay and Display)
Route terrain	Mainly clear paths and tracks over farmland and rough mountainside. Short sections on quiet lanes
Ordnance Survey maps	Landranger 160 (Brecon Beacons), Explorer OL12 (Brecon Beacons National Park – Western & Central area)

GPS waypoints

- 🖉 SN 977 262
- Ⓐ SN 970 253
- Ⓑ SN 959 259
- Ⓒ SN 956 264
- Ⓓ SN 944 257
- Ⓔ SN 949 280
- Ⓕ SN 954 278

From the open, spacious common land of Mynydd Illtud at the start and finish of the walk there are splendid views of the main ridge of the Brecon Beacons, and there are more open and extensive views from the slopes of Cefn Llechid, especially over the Usk Valley. As a contrast there is the pleasant wooded valley of Cwm Camlais and easy and enjoyable walking along a wide drove road. This walk provides varied scenery and grand views for relatively little effort as there are no steep climbs or difficult terrain to be negotiated.

The Brecon Beacons Mountain Centre, opened in 1966, is situated 1,100 feet (335m) up on Mynydd Illtud, a large area of open common which gives grand panoramic views over the mountains.

🖉 Begin by turning left out of the entrance along a road and at a T-junction leave the road by keeping straight ahead and continuing along a gravel track which keeps along the edge of the rather marshy common, near a wire fence and line of trees on the left. After ¾ mile, just after the top of the hill and before a stile on the left, 250 yds short of some farm buildings, turn right Ⓐ onto a very obvious broad, grassy track. This heads across the common in a north-westerly direction, between the two marshy areas of Traeth Mawr and Traeth Bach, to reach a road just to the right of a large pool Ⓑ.

Cross the road, continue along the broad, grassy, enclosed track opposite – it is likely that this was an old drove road – and after nearly ½ mile take the first turning on the left, marked by a post Ⓒ. Go through a wooden gate, head downhill along a hedge-lined, enclosed path that leads down to a lane. Turn left along this narrow, winding lane for $^3/_4$ mile, following it around several sharp bends to reach the A4215.

A few yards before the road turn right **D** through a gate onto a sunken path between hedge banks and follow it gently uphill through a series of gates and stiles, eventually emerging onto the open, windswept Cefn Llechid Common. Keep straight ahead at a crossroads of grassy tracks on a waymarked bridleway and continue through bracken, enjoying the extensive all-round views. On the skyline to the left the triangulation pillar marks the highest point on the common 1,314 feet (400m); it is worth a brief detour for the magnificent views. After passing several pools the route starts to descend, by a hedge bank and wire fence on the right, with superb views ahead over the Usk Valley.

Leave the track to the right to go through a wooden gate, a few yards to the left of a fence corner, and continue quite steeply downhill along a sunken path, by a wire fence on the right, passing through a succession of gates and stiles to reach a narrow lane **E**. Turn right along it for $^1/_2$ mile, heading downhill, and where the lane bends left in front of Cwm-Camlais-uchaf Farm **F** keep ahead through the farmyard, bearing right through a metal gate at the far end to continue along a winding track. The track soon joins the lovely, tree-lined stream of Cwm Camlais which rushes over rocks and small falls. Turn left over a footbridge at a

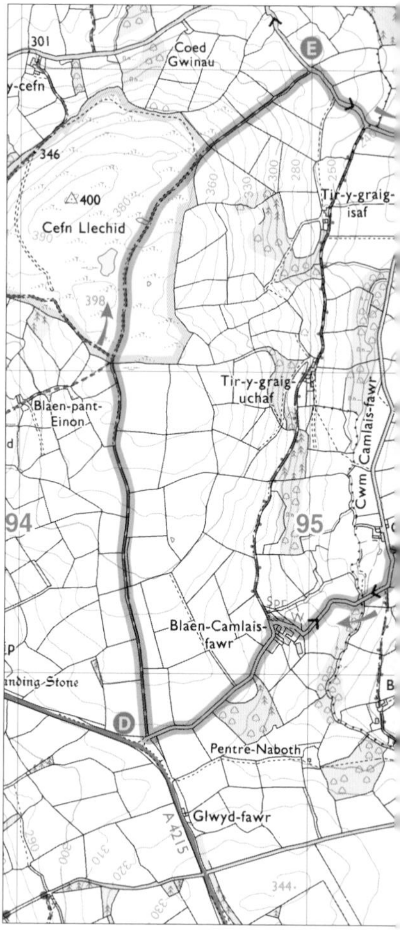

Trees above Cwm Camlais

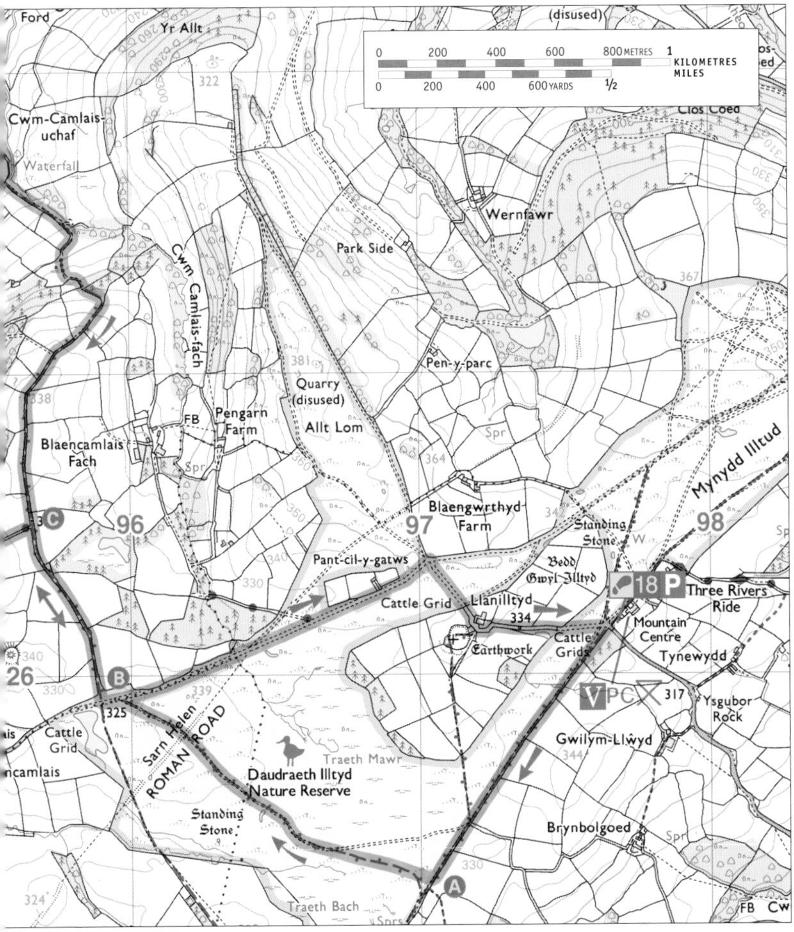

SCALE 1:25 000 or 2½ INCHES to 1 MILE 4CM to 1KM

confluence of streams, bear right and head across to join an enclosed path. Bear left to follow this path uphill through woodland above the valley of Cwm Camlais-fach. Go through a metal gate, and then another, and turn right to continue along an enclosed path between hedged banks.

A few yards after the hedge banks peter out, with a gate directly ahead, look out for where the sunken path reappears on the left and follow it uphill to a gate on the edge of a plantation. Go through the gate to walk along the right inside edge of the plantation, by a wire fence on the right, and just before reaching the corner of it turn right through another gate to continue along an uphill sunken path. Later the path levels out and continues as a wide, green, tree-lined enclosed track – the old drove road again – follow it through a series of gates and stiles, later picking up part of the outward route and continuing to the road B. This is easy and most enjoyable walking, with the magnificent panorama of the Brecon Beacons spread out ahead of you all the while.

Leave the outward route at the road by turning left along it across Illtud Common and after ¾ mile turn right along a lane signposted to the mountain centre. Follow it back to the start, passing to the left of the ruined church of Llanilltyd.

Hay Bluff and Twmpa

		GPS waypoints
Start	Hay Bluff	SO 239 373
Distance	6 miles (9.8km)	Ⓐ SO 244 366
Height gain	1,390 feet (425m)	Ⓑ SO 235 351
Approximate time	3 hours	Ⓒ SO 220 346
Parking	Free car park beside stone circle on the Gospel Pass road between Hay-on-Wye and Abergavenny	Ⓓ SO 231 356
Route terrain	Clear paths over high mountains and open moorland, with a return leg along a quiet lane	
Ordnance Survey maps	Landranger 161 (The Black Mountains), Explorer OL13 (Brecon Beacons National Park – Eastern area)	

The adjacent open expanses of Hay Bluff and Twmpa – the alternative name for the latter is Lord Hereford's Knob – are the most northerly peaks of the Black Mountains and from them there are extensive views of the long ridges of the mountains and over the Wye Valley to the hills of mid Wales. The walk involves two ascents: the first to the summit of Hay Bluff (2,220ft/677m) is steep, the second to the summit of Twmpa (2263ft/689m) is easier and more gradual. It is best to choose a fine, clear day for this walk, to enjoy the grand views to the full and because otherwise route-finding in such open terrain could be difficult.

From the car park and stone circle cross the road and head uphill across grass to the summit of Hay Bluff which lies directly ahead. At about half height, you'll meet a good path rising up from your left; turn right onto Offa's Dyke Path and follow it to the top. Turn left onto a good gravel path and follow this to the triangulation pillar Ⓐ from which the views over the Black Mountains, Brecon Beacons, Wye Valley and hills of mid-Wales are magnificent. Now retrace your steps back along the path to the top of the initial climb and instead of descending again, keep straight ahead to continue along the edge of the escarpment of Ffynnon y Parc, heading towards the prominent steep face of Twmpa. The track eventually descends to the road and parking area at Gospel Pass Ⓑ. Cross

The glorious view from the summit of Twmpa

the road and keep straight ahead to follow a continuation path easily up onto the hillside on the other side of the pass, this now leads onto Twmpa. Near the top the path passes between two piles of stones – remnants of cairns – and continues to a third one which marks the summit, another superb viewpoint. From here continue along the edge of the escarpment, bearing slightly left and gently descending. Later the broad, grassy path levels out; follow it almost to the rim of the chasm ahead.

Turn right here (C) onto a clear path which heads steeply downhill. You'll reach a deep groove, after which the original bridleway bends around to the left, but you need to keep straight ahead, descending steeply, until the ground levels at a junction with a clear cross path, approximately 200 yds from the fence below, and directly below two small clumps of trees. Turn right onto this, which climbs slightly to start with, and continue beneath the obvious nose of Twmpa. Later you join a wider path, bearing right and still keeping below the curving slopes of Twmpa. From here there are particularly dramatic views of Twmpa on the right and the long ridge of Hay Bluff ahead.

On joining a narrow lane turn right along it to walk through a pleasant area of trees, ford two streams at a left-hand bend (D) and follow the lane for just over 1 mile to get back to the starting point. This is a delightful, unspoilt, old-fashioned country lane which appears to be used more by walkers and riders than vehicles; it heads gently uphill across open country below Hay Bluff. ●

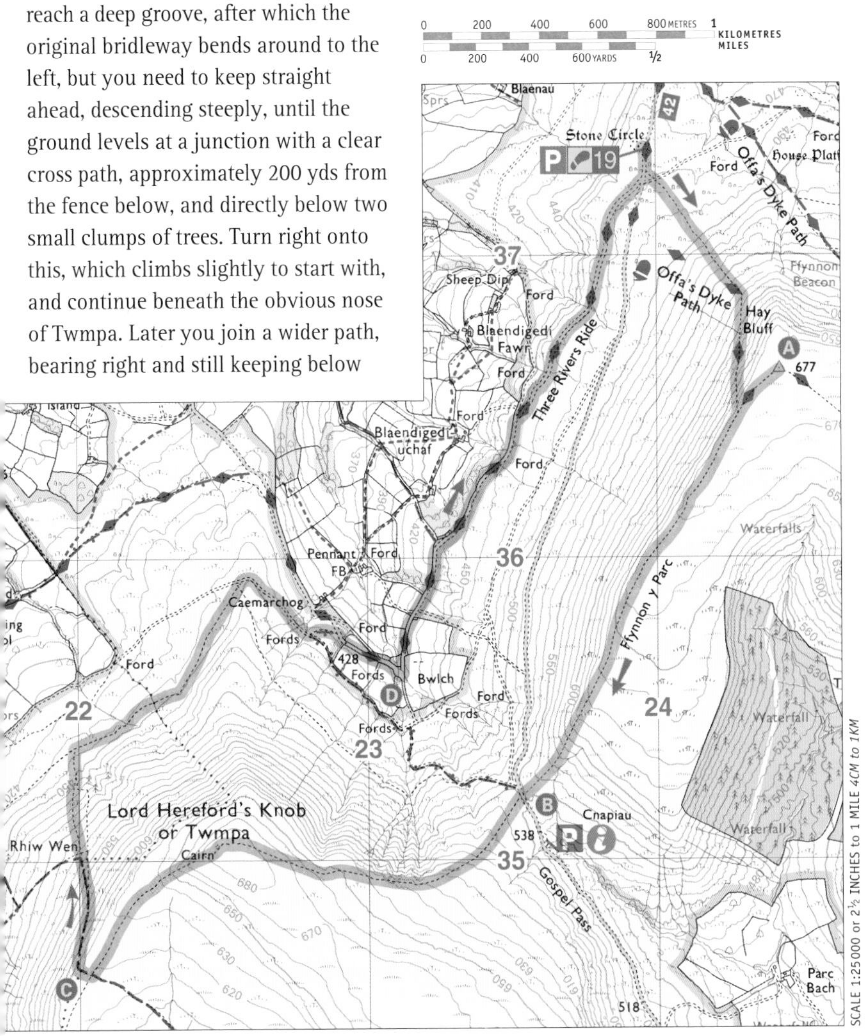

The Vale of Ewyas

Start	Llanthony Priory
Distance	6 miles (9.7km)
Height gain	1,210 feet (370m)
Approximate time	3 hours
Parking	Car park at Llanthony Priory (free)
Route terrain	Clear paths over high mountains and less clear paths over farmland. A long section on a very quiet road
Ordnance Survey maps	Landranger 161 (The Black Mountains), Explorer OL13 (Brecon Beacons National Park – Eastern area)

GPS waypoints

- SO 289 278
- Ⓐ SO 285 279
- Ⓑ SO 270 299
- Ⓒ SO 268 296
- Ⓓ SO 273 266

The Vale of Ewyas, a narrow, remote, steep-sided valley on the eastern edge of the Black Mountains, provides a romantic, secluded setting for the ruins of Llanthony Priory. Initially the walk follows a pleasant track northwards along the bottom of the valley before turning westwards to cross the River Honddu and climb onto open moorland. A delightful ramble follows, along the western slopes of the valley to Bal-Bach, a fine viewpoint over both the vale of Ewyas and the neighbouring Grwyne Fawr Valley. On the final descent the priory ruins are in sight most of the time. This highly scenic and quite energetic walk is best done on a fine day as in misty conditions route-finding on the open moorland stretch could be difficult.

The austere-looking ruins of Llanthony Priory perfectly match their setting in the peaceful, lonely vale of Ewyas enclosed by the bare slopes of the Black Mountains. The Augustinian priory was founded in the early 12th century and much of the late 12th and early 13th-century church survives, notably the west front, the north arcade of the nave, the central tower and parts of the east end. Little remains of the domestic buildings, although the small parish church nearby incorporates the monks' infirmary. Uniquely, the south west tower of the priory church is now part of the **Abbey Hotel**, surely one of the most unusual hotel sites in the country.

Leave the car park by walking between the priory ruins on the right and the church on the left. Go through a gate straight ahead, and follow the waymark across the field in the direction of Capel-y-ffin, making for a gate to the left of a barn – formerly the priory gate-house – onto a road and bear right along it, passing the **Half Moon Inn**. Where the road bears left to Capel-y-ffyn, keep straight ahead Ⓐ. After passing through a gate, with a drive up to the right, the lane becomes a tree-lined path for a while, before reverting to a tarmac track at the next gate. Along this stretch

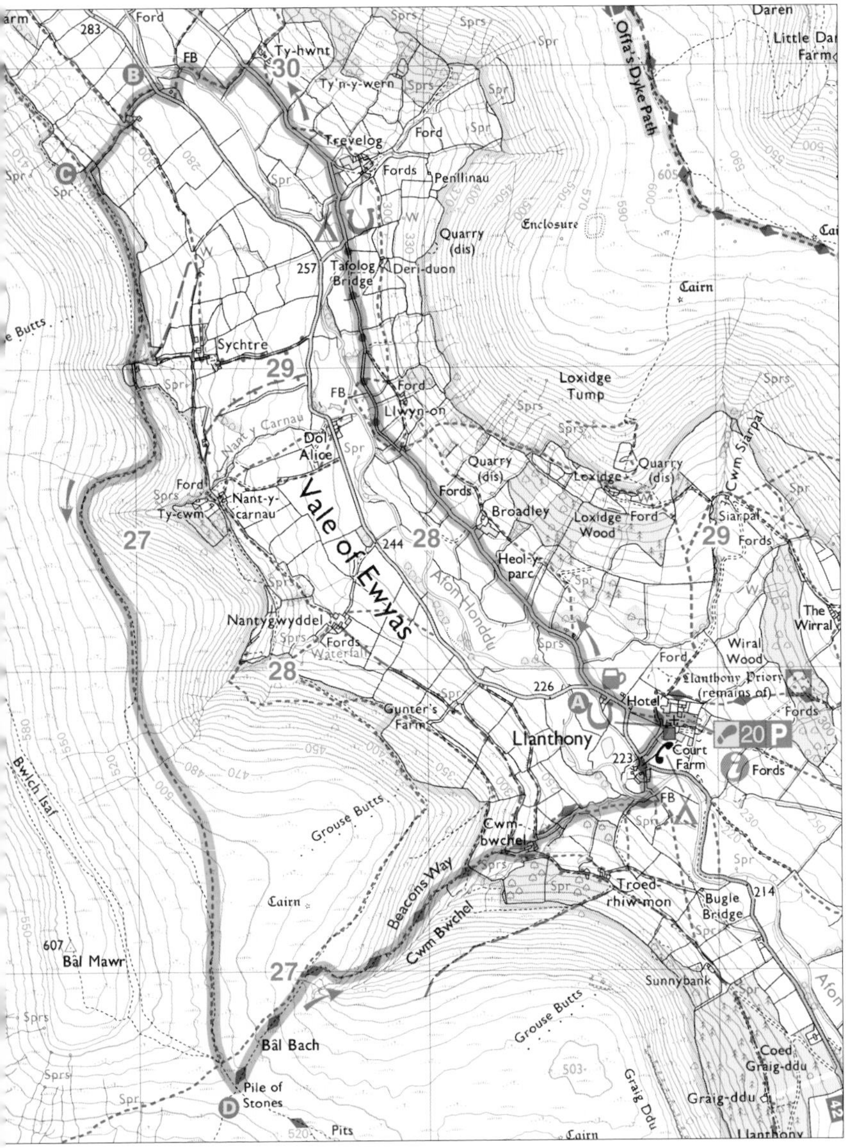

SCALE 1:25 000 or 2½ INCHES to 1 MILE 4CM to 1KM

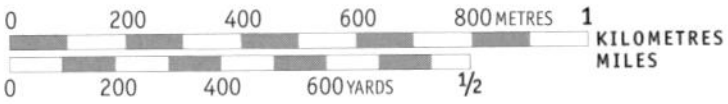

there are lovely views in front looking towards the head of the valley.

At a public footpath sign to Hay Road turn left through a metal gate and head downhill along the left-hand edge of the field, by a wire fence bordering a stream on the left, later bearing right away from the field edge and going through a gap in a line of trees. Continue down to the bottom and bear right to a stile by some sheep pens.

Cross this and continue for a few paces to a footbridge over the River Honddu. Cross this and climb a stile above it to continue to a gate and then the road.

Turn right and after a few yards, where the road bears slightly right, turn left **B** up some steps, climb a stile and head uphill along the left-hand edge of

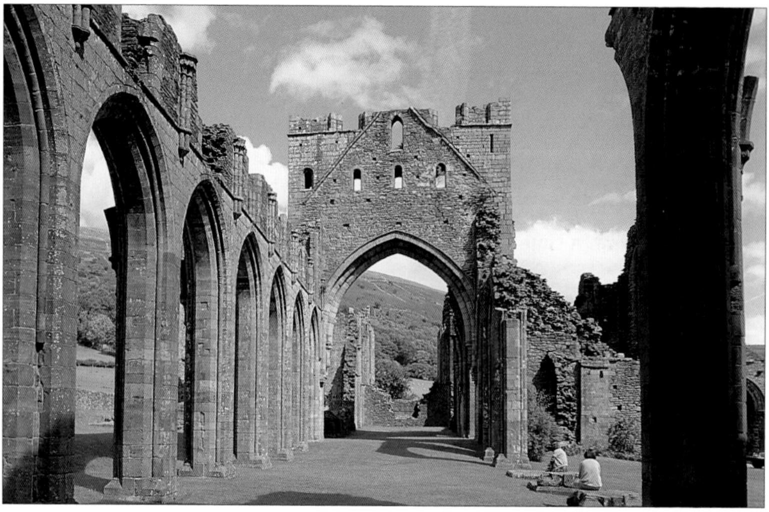

Llanthony Priory

a field, by a wooded gully and stream on the left. Near the top of the field, bear left over a stile, with a house to your left, and then turn immediately right to walk steeply up the right-hand edge of the field with a bramble-filled gulley to your left. At the top, climb a stile and turn left **C** to keep alongside a wire fence on the left, soon picking up a clear path which can be seen a few yards to the right. This path winds along the bottom edge of open moorland, keeping roughly parallel with the wire fence on the left. There are superb views over the valley and at times the ruins of Llanthony Priory can be glimpsed.

Where the path forks above a farm building, take the right-hand, upper path which heads away from the wire fence to join a wider, clearer path. Bear left along it, go through a metal gate and keep ahead to pass through another one. The path now starts to climb and becomes more rocky as first it bends right above the edge of a steep valley, and then it bears left across the head of the valley to continue across the lovely, open, heathery moorland on the western slopes of the Vale of Ewyas.

Make for the cairn that can be seen on the skyline ahead; this is Bal-Bach where there is a junction of tracks and paths and a view to the right over the forested Grwyne Fawr Valley **D**. Here turn left downhill along a broad, well-used path. At a fork take the right-hand path, shortly turning right and heading downhill along the left-hand side of the narrow, steep-sided valley of Cwm Bwchel. *Be careful as the path is steep and rocky.* As it descends there are glorious views of the priory ruins in front. At a footpath sign keep ahead in the Llanthony direction, climb a stile and continue downhill to climb another. Keep ahead, go through a gate, with the farm to your right, and continue past a stile, where the path bears left away from the fence to a waymark post in a gap in the trees ahead. Continue down to another stile and climb it then turn right to climb another. Take the foot-bridge over the stream and keep ahead to another stile. Now turn left to drop down to a gate in the corner. Go through this and follow the path down to cross an iron footbridge over the river. Turn right along a track through a farmyard to a road. Cross the road and follow the lane opposite to return to the priory. ●

Talgarth and Mynydd Troed

		GPS waypoints
Start	Talgarth	(start) SO 152 336
Distance	8 miles (13km)	Ⓐ SO 146 334
Height gain	1,050 feet (320m)	Ⓑ SO 144 325
Approximate time	4 hours	Ⓒ SO 152 304
Parking	Free car park on the A479	Ⓓ SO 160 295
Route terrain	Mainly clear paths and tracks over farmland and rough mountainside. Short sections on quiet lanes	Ⓔ SO 150 315
		Ⓕ SO 142 321
Ordnance Survey maps	Landranger 161 (The Black Mountains), Explorer OL13 (Brecon Beacons National Park – Eastern area)	

Mynydd Troed sits in a kind of no man's land between the main massif of the Black Mountains, and the lower-lying ground that surrounds Llangorse Lake. It's a shapely peak, especially when seen from the north, where its sharp northern ridge and slender summit conspire to give it an almost pyramidical appearance. This walk approaches the mountain from this direction, deflecting easily around the peak itself on good paths. It then returns to the small town of Talgarth via the impressive Penyrwrlodd Long Cairn.

Leave the car park via an exit in the bottom corner that leads onto the main road, at the same end as the main entrance. Cross the road and turn left then right through a gate towards the rugby pitch. Turn immediately left onto a track and follow it past a barn and through a gate. Continue diagonally across the next field to a stile and then continue ahead on a rough, hedged track that then veers left to a gate onto the road.

Turn right and then left Ⓐ, just before crossing a bridge, onto a signed footpath. Follow this around the edge of the field and through a stile then continue ahead, keeping the River Llynfi to your right, to the far end of the field, where you'll join a lane. Turn right and then left onto a drive, marked Pont Nichol. Walk up the drive and pass beneath the house, which sits on the site of the old railway crossing. Now fork left to a stile that leads into a wood and follow the path through the woodland and up to another stile that leads onto the B4560, close to College Farm Ⓑ.

Turn right to walk along the road and into Trefecca village. Trefecca was the home of Hywel Harris, one of the leaders of the Welsh Methodist Revival and the settlement he founded, now known as Trefecca College, is passed later on the walk. Leave the village and then take the no through road on the left, which leads up to Trefecca Fawr. Follow the lane around to the right and then continue through Felin Cwm Dingle to a sharp left-hand bend, where you should go straight ahead through a gate into a field.

Continue with the wood on your left and go through another gate and up through the next field to a stile. Cross this and turn right, over a stream, and then left to follow a line of trees up and then right, aiming all the time towards the farm buildings. Continue to a gate in front of the farm but do not go through, instead turn left to keep the hedge to your right, and walk up to a stile that leads onto the road **C**. Turn right to walk past Whole House Farm and continue past the farmhouse to a track on the left. Follow this up through three fields and upon entering the third, bear half left to aim for the bottom left corner, where you join a lane. Turn right and walk past the turn to Garn y Castell and around a sharp left-hand bend. Now keep your eyes open for a narrow path that leads into a copse on the left. Follow this path through two gates and out onto the open ground at the foot of Mynydd Troed **D**.

Turn left and follow the obvious track along the foot of the mountain until it dips leftwards towards a gate that leads onto a road. Turn left onto the lane and then turn right at the next junction and continue past Penyrheol and Trewalkin farms. Continue for another 100 yds and bear left, through a gate. Now head across the field towards the left-hand end of the farm ahead. Cross a stile and go straight across a track and then over another stile, to enter another field. Keep to the right to another stile and then head diagonally right, over the brow of the hill and down to the far corner, where you'll see another stile beneath a small plantation of evergreens. Cross this and then a stile on the right to enter the site of the Penyrwrlodd Long Cairn **E**.

Looking across at Y Grib from Mynydd Troed

This is an amazing example of a long barrow burial cairn, which despite its colossal size was only discovered in 1972. Human remains suggest it was constructed around 3800BC, which makes it one of the oldest cairns in southern Britain. Among the many finds it has yielded is a small length of hollowed out sheep bone with holes drilled in it – possibly a very early musical instrument.

Go back over the stile and turn right down to another stile. Continue with the hedge on your right and pass through a gate to continue to a cluster of buildings. Keep these to your left and locate a path that ducks into bushes on the right. Continue down, with the hedge to your right, to a gate and stile close to a new barn. Turn left onto the lane and follow it down past Trefecca College to the B4560 **F**.

Cross the road and continue down the lane opposite, which turns into a steep, stony track and drops to cross the dismantled railway. Bear left then right to cross a footbridge over the Afon Llynfi. Now head up the steep bank ahead to join a lane by the farm buildings at Tredustan Hall. Turn right onto the lane and follow it easily back towards Talgarth, taking a right and then a left at the two junctions.

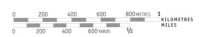

0 200 400 600 800 METRES 1 KILOMETRES
0 200 400 600 YARDS 1/2 MILES

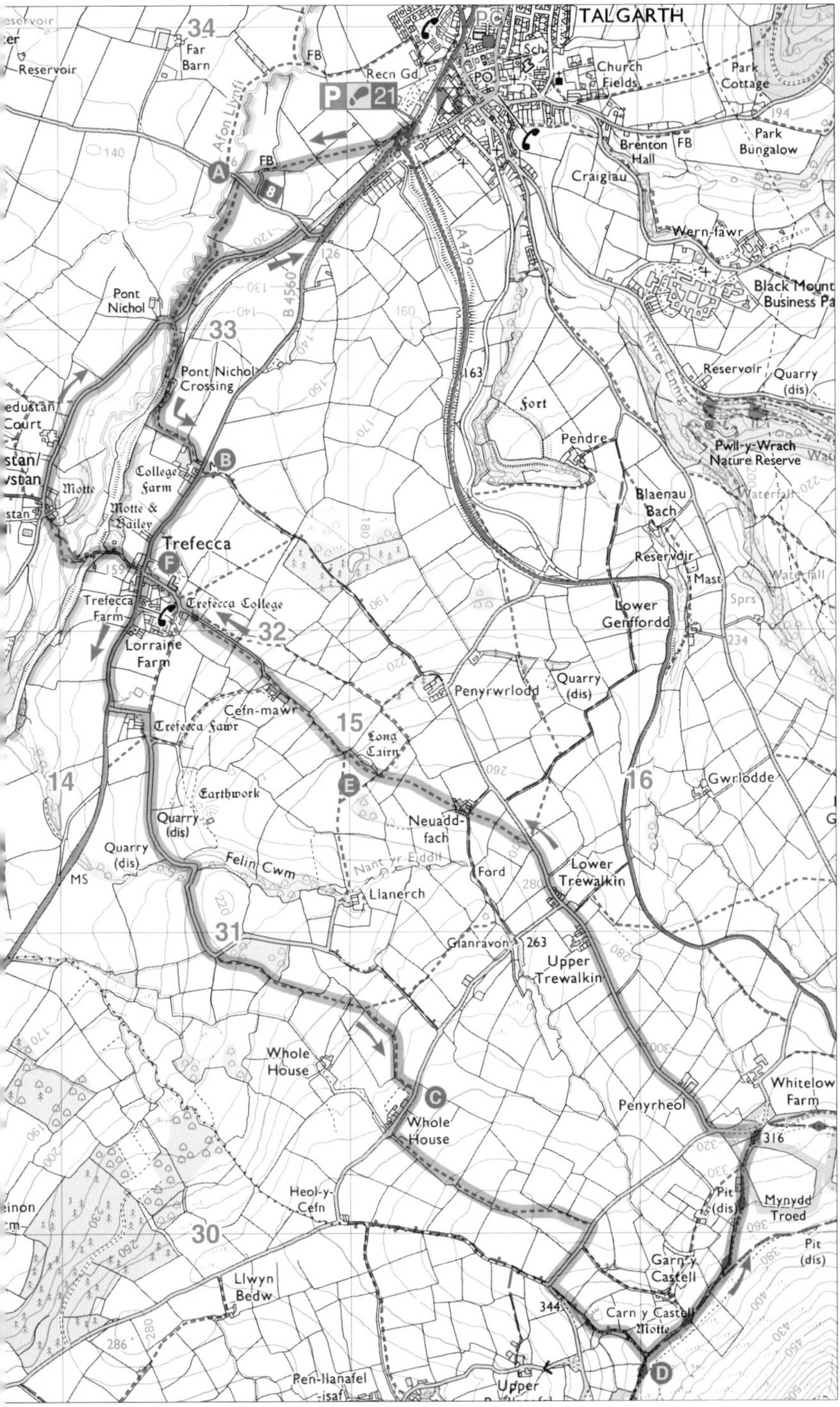

SCALE 1:25000 or 2½ INCHES to 1 MILE 4CM to 1KM

Llyn y Fan Fach and the Carmarthen Fans

Start	Near Llanddeusant
Distance	6 miles (9.7km)
Height gain	2,130 feet (650m)
Approximate time	4 hours
Parking	Free parking off a track leading on from dead-end lane east from Llandeusant
Route terrain	A mixture of faint and clear paths over high mountains. Some steep going. Easy return along a broad track
Ordnance Survey maps	Landranger 160 (Brecon Beacons), Explorer OL12 (Brecon Beacons National Park – Western area)

GPS waypoints

- SN 799 238
- Ⓐ SN 814 237
- Ⓑ SN 821 223
- Ⓒ SN 811 218
- Ⓓ SN 797 220
- Ⓔ SN 803 220

The Black Mountain (singular) is the western-most massif of the Brecon Beacons National Park and is often described as its last surviving wilderness, with sweeping, craggy escarpments that tower commandingly above glistening lakes, and a peaty upland plateau that bears few paths. This walk links a good waterworks track with a spectacular ridge-top path to create a short but extremely rewarding tour of the high escarpments at the western edge of the range, often known as the Carmarthen Fans.

Bannau Sir Gaer and Llyn y Fan Fach

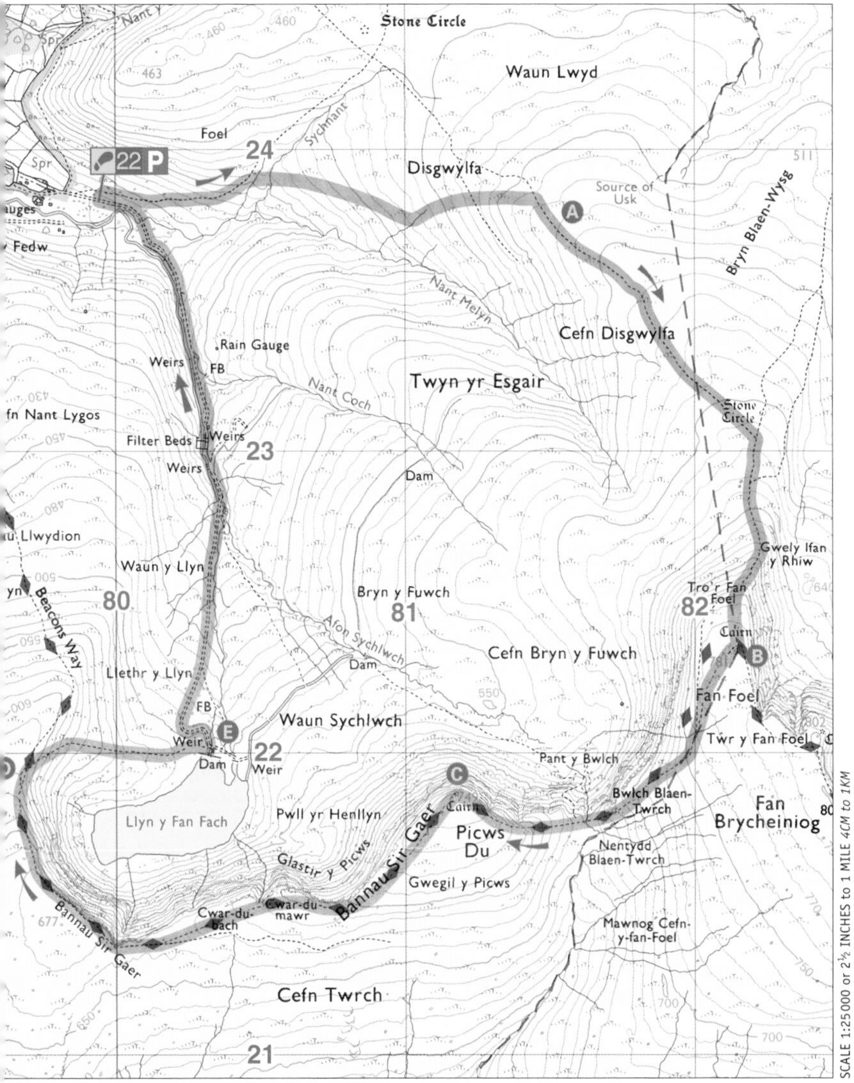

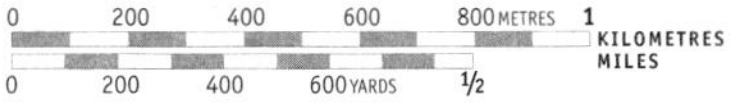

From the car park, cross the access track and climb the steep hillside almost directly above a small signpost. At the top of this short, steep slope, the ground levels and you should locate a faint path that contours eastwards around the hillside. Follow this through the gorse, climbing slightly all the time, and then drop to cross a stream. Keep ahead on the same trajectory and you'll drop to cross a bigger stream, this one the Sychnant brook.

Leaving this behind and keeping the deep gorge of the Nant Melyn beneath you to the right, stay on the path as it contours just south of east around the hillside. Stay with the path, which does start to become faint until you reach a small stream gully. Here, turn left and climb alongside it all the way to the crest of the broad ridge above and to your left. You'll cross a path near the top but ignore this and you'll find another on the crest itself Ⓐ. Onto it, bear right and track along the ridge top towards the mountains on the horizon.

You're now aiming for the steep and obvious spur of Fan Foel, which lies south east of you just over 1 mile away. Follow the main track which is faint in places over Waun Lwyd and then, as the ridge starts to narrow, keep to the crest where you'll meet a very distinct path coming up from your left. Continue towards the steep spur and follow the path sharply up it to a cairn and stone circle on the grassy plateau above Ⓑ. This is Fan Foel, and although it's a few feet smaller than Fan Brycheiniog, just a short distance to the south, it still makes a magnificent viewpoint.

From the cairn, bear right to follow the edge along, and drop easily at first, and then steeply, into the deep col of Bwlch Blaen-Twrch, which marks the boundary between Powys and Carmarthenshire. From here, climb steeply up the hillside ahead to the summit cairn of Bannau Sir Gaer Ⓒ – another wonderful viewpoint. Stay with the path and continue with the escarpment edge to your right, above precipitous cliffs, into a small saddle, directly above Llyn y Fan Fach. Climb slightly again and then continue around the lake until you see a good path

The lofty escarpment of Bannau Sir Gaer

dropping down a grassy spur towards the dam D. Take this and drop to the lake itself E.

Llyn y Fan Fach is often referred to as the magic lake after a mythical story of a lady of the lake. The lady, both beautiful and wise, with special healing powers, appeared regularly to a shepherd boy named Rhiwallon. He fell for her and persuaded her to marry him. She agreed, but only on the condition that he should never strike her with iron. They duly married and had a son before Rhiwallon did strike her with iron and, true to her word, the lady vanished back into the black waters, taking their livestock with her. Their son, named after his father, went on to become a great healer. This is most likely a twist on a tale that is told in many places and is thought to reflect on the advance of the Iron Age in Britain and of the Bronze Age people's distrust of their strange new neighbours. It's likely that a Bronze Age lady would have had a good understanding of healing using natural medicines but what's particularly interestingly about this version of the story is that much later on, there actually was a line of successful physicians operating from nearby Myddfai.

From the dam, pick up the well-surfaced track that heads back downhill. This will lead you past the waterworks filter beds, which you pass on the right, and back to the car park.

Grwyne Fawr

Start	Pont Cadwgan
Distance	7½ miles (12.1km)
Height gain	1,720 feet (525m)
Approximate time	4 hours
Parking	Forestry Commission car park at Pont Cadwgan
Route terrain	A real mix of forest roads, well-marked footpaths over sheep pasture and less well-established footpaths over high mountains. *Best tackled in good visibility*
Ordnance Survey maps	Landranger 161 (The Black Mountains), Explorer OL13 (Brecon Beacons National Park – Eastern area)

GPS waypoints

- Start: SO 266 251
- A: SO 268 237
- B: SO 260 237
- C: SO 262 226
- D: SO 278 224
- E: SO 283 226
- F: SO 281 235

The Grwyne Fawr Valley is one of a series of long, narrow, parallel valleys that separates the ridges of the Black Mountains. The walk begins by heading uphill through the conifers of Mynydd Du Forest on the western side of the valley, emerging onto open moorland to reach the grand viewpoint of Crug Mawr (1,805ft /550m). A descent to the delightful, secluded Partrishow church is followed by a high-level return route along the eastern side of the valley. Forest, moorland, wooded valley and extensive views all combine to create a most varied and satisfying walk, and although there is some climbing along the route, none of it is steep or strenuous.

Leave the car park, cross the bridge (Pont Cadwgan) onto the road and take the forest track opposite which bears left and climbs steadily. Follow the track around a right-hand curve, keep ahead to a crossroads of tracks and bear left to continue along a winding track signed to Fford Las Fawr through a pleasant area of mixed woodland. Go through a gate, keep ahead to a farm, turn left at the end of the farm buildings, by a public bridleway sign, and continue between trees for 100 yds to a clear path leading right **A**, steeply uphill. Follow this, keeping straight ahead across two forest tracks, until you reach a gate at the top that leads onto open moorland **B**. Turn left onto a path that runs along the forest edge to the corner of the plantation, from where a triangulation pillar can be seen ahead on the summit of Crug Mawr. Bear half right for a few paces to join a clear path that heads towards it across the heathery moorland, ascending gently. From the summit **C** there is a magnificent panoramic view that includes the Sugar Loaf, Ysgyryd Fawr, the Grwyne Fawr valley, the western ridges of the Black Mountains, the Usk Valley and the main Brecon Beacons beyond.

Retrace your steps to the corner of the forest, bear right and follow a path that winds downhill, keeping roughly parallel to the edge of the trees and later dipping below them. Where the path levels out pick up and continue along a pleasant, grassy track that curves to the right, following the bottom edge of Crug Mawr. Go through a gate, head down an enclosed, stony track to a lane, bear right and follow it downhill around some sharp bends to Partrishow church, ignoring a stile marked Beacons Way and continuing to the ornate gates **D** where you turn left into the churchyard. This is a delightful, unspoilt, secluded church in a lovely, remote mountain setting, and is particularly noted for its superb 15th-century carved oak screen. It also has a medieval painting of a skeleton on the west wall of the nave

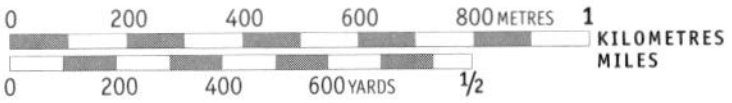

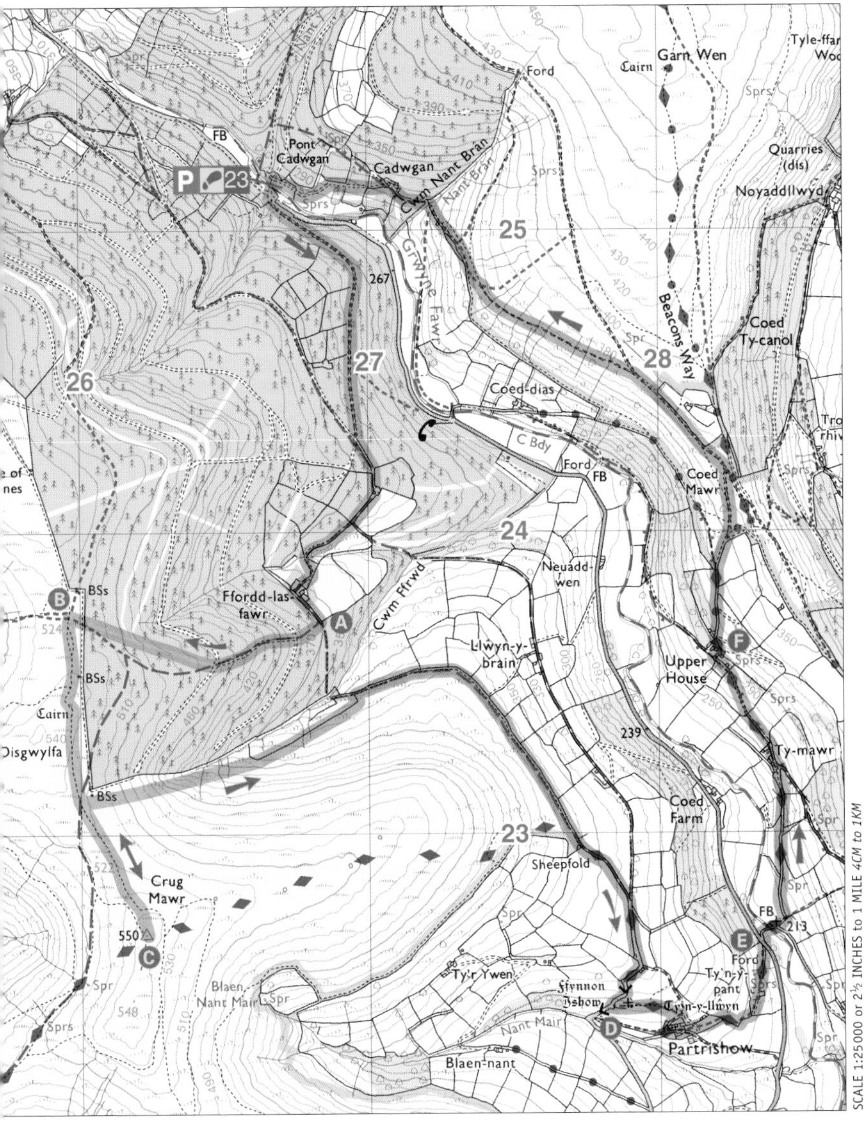

and a parish chest hewn from a solid tree trunk.

Pass to the right of the church, go through a gate at the far end of the churchyard and continue across a sloping field. Bear right on joining a track, follow it around a sharp right-hand bend and continue down to the attractive 15th-century buildings of Tyn-y-llwyn Farm. Turn left, passing beneath the farmhouse, and go through a metal gate on the left, above the drive and next to a small outhouse, to walk across a field to a stile. Climb it, bear right downhill across the next field to climb another stile, bear left and continue downhill, passing between two ruined buildings and on down a most attractive tree-lined path to climb a stile onto a road (E).

Cross over the road, take the downhill tarmac track opposite, which is sign-posted 'Tabernacle Chapel', turn right to cross the stream and continue, passing to the right of the chapel. Shortly afterwards the track bends to the left and climbs gently along the eastern side of the valley. Go through a metal gate, keep ahead, pass to the right of a farm and continue, going through several more metal gates, up to the next farm, Upper House.

Go through a metal gate into the farmyard, turn right (F), in the direction of a yellow waymark, between the farmhouse and a barn, then turn left and continue up, going through another metal gate. Walk along an uphill track, passing through a metal gate onto open moorland, and bear slightly right to keep alongside a wall on the right. Where the wall turns to the right keep ahead along an obvious grassy track towards the ridge in front.

On meeting a broader track just before a group of conifers bear left onto it to continue along the side of the valley – this is a superb high level walk with grand views. About 50 yds after a fence on the right ends there is a fork; take the left-hand, narrower path which eventually descends into the valley of Cwm Nant Brân, meeting a wall on the left and keeping alongside it downhill. Cross a small stream, go through a gate and then continue along a wooded path gently uphill to a farm. Turn left to pass between gateposts and, ignoring a waymark to the right, follow the track ahead which descends between thick conifers to the starting point. ●

Partrishow church

Waterfalls Walk

Start	Cwm Porth
Distance	9 miles (14.5km)
Height gain	2,100 feet (640m)
Approximate time	5 hours
Parking	Pay and Display car park, on minor road 1 mile (1.6km) south of Ystradfellte
Route terrain	Clear but rough paths with some very steep and exposed sections and a slippery walk beneath a waterfall
Dog friendly	Great care needed near the steep drops and waterfalls
Ordnance Survey maps	Landranger 160 (Brecon Beacons), Explorer OL12 (Brecon Beacons National Park – Western area)

GPS waypoints

- SN 928 124
- Ⓐ SN 924 109
- Ⓑ SN 928 099
- Ⓒ SN 910 079
- Ⓓ SN 900 076
- Ⓔ SN 898 091
- Ⓕ SN 907 105
- Ⓖ SN 912 116
- Ⓗ SN 918 116

There can be few more exhilarating and satisfying walks than this. On the southern edge of Fforest Fawr, where the sandstone that underlies most of the National Park gives way to limestone, the rivers Mellte, Hepste, Pyrddin and Nedd Fechan plunge over a series of waterfalls, the highest concentration of falls in Wales. All are spectacular but probably the most exciting part of the walk comes when you walk behind the great sheet of water at Sgŵd yr Eira. The walk is lengthy and quite energetic, with plenty of ascents and descents and some fairly difficult sections over rocky terrain and muddy paths, some above very steep drops. Take your time and watch your step, for this is a walk to be enjoyed to the full and worth taking slowly.

Leave the car park and go through the left-hand of two entrances opposite (signed footpath). Walk past a stile, which is signed 'Cavers only' and go through a kissing-gate to drop to the grassy banks of the river. Now bear left to follow the stony and often muddy path along the side of the river, passing through two gates and rising and dropping a few times. Eventually you'll pass a footbridge over the river, at which point you drop to cross a small brook and then climb steeply into a wood, with a fence on your left. At the top, keep ahead towards another fence a few paces away and follow this down to the viewing area above the waterfall of Sgŵd Clun-gwyn Ⓐ.

The next section is steep and rocky and there are some very steep drops. If you do not feel confident about tackling it, head back uphill the way you came to the edge of the conifer plantation, and then bear right and right again to follow red-topped markers through the wood to Sgŵd yr Eira Ⓑ.

From here, turn effectively left, to walk past a green warning notice and then down and up to another. Now continue on the narrow path which contours around the steep hillside above a very steep drop. At one point it dips beneath overhanging cliffs and, shortly after this, it drops very steeply to the right to the viewing area close to the second waterfall, Sgŵd Isaf Clun-gwyn. *This section is steep and slippery so take great care.*

From the waterfall, continue along the bank of the river and head downstream, past a path that goes up to the left, until you reach another waterfall, Sgŵd Pannwr. Turn left here, and follow a faint path steeply uphill, where it joins another coming in from the left. Continue upwards, over a short boardwalk section, and up to a T-junction, where you should turn right to follow red-topped posts. Follow the path easily around the hillside to a junction marked with a tall fingerpost. Turn right, down a steep flight of steps which twist and turn sharply, and follow the steps down to the bottom of the gorge.

Turn left to Sgŵd yr Eira – *take care, the path is difficult in places.* Now comes the most exciting part of the walk; you turn right to pass behind the fall **B**. *Be careful – the rocks are slippery, and if the falls are very full they create a strong back draft which can make things very wet.* On the other side climb quite steeply along a rocky, curving path, turning sharp right at a yellow waymark to continue twisting and turning up steps. At the top turn right at a public footpath sign, following directions to Pontneddfechan and Craig y Ddinas, and continue along the top of the gorge. Soon the path bears left away from the river to continue through a mixture of woodland and more open moorland; keep following the regular waymarks and footpath signs to Craig y Ddinas (Dinas Rock). At a public footpath sign for Dinas Rock car park, keep straight ahead along the broad ridge of Craig y Ddinas, above two rivers **C**. Soon the path heads downhill to the car park. Cross the road and follow the footpath opposite that leads along the banks of river to a bridge. Turn right to cross this and then turn left to follow the road into Pontneddfechan.

Walk through the village and in front of the **Angel** pub turn right **D**. This is a delightful section, keeping beside the rushing waters of the Afon Nedd Fechan. Climb a stile and shortly afterwards the track narrows to a path; follow it as far as a footbridge just beyond the confluence of the Afon Nedd Fechan and the Afon Pyrddin **E**. Turn right over the bridge to a footpath sign on the other side and turn left for a short detour to view Sgŵd Gwladus, which some would consider the most beautiful of all the falls in its lovely, wooded amphitheatre.

Retrace your steps to the footbridge and keep ahead to another one a few yards ahead. Do not cross it but continue above the left bank of the River Neath, following the footpath sign to Pont Melin-fach. This is another lovely section of the walk, passing several small falls and with fine views up the river. Turn right over a footbridge and continue by the river, passing Sgŵd Ddwli, eventually climbing a stile and bearing left through a car park to a bridge (Pont Melin-fach) **F**. Cross the bridge and take the stile on the left. Immediately, turn right up a narrow path, clamber up over roots and then swing left with the path to trace a course through the woods. In 400 yds it drops almost to river level; here keep right, up a stony path-cum-streambed. In 150 yds you'll pass a redundant,

0 200 400 600 800 METRES 1 KILOMETRES
MILES
0 200 400 600 YARDS 1/2
Enclosure
Shake Holes
Dyffryn-Nedd
297
Coetgae
Plasydarren
Plas-y-darren
24
Spr
Cave
Pot Hole
Pen-y
Caves
Cwm Porth
Pant-y-llwyn
317
297
300
Nant y Carad
Nant-y-carred
Gwaun Bryn-bwch
302
Waterfall
Ford
Fire Tower
332
Waterfall
12
Pwll Du
Waterfalls
Gors-wen
Tref-garn
FB
Fall
Pont-Rhyd-y-cnau
292
280
270
Bryn-bwch
Afon Mellte
Ford
Cairns
Coed y Rhaiadr
Hendre-bolon
FB
260
250
240
Fords
Waterfalls
Gwern-pitoed
11
Ford
Heol-fawr
264
Sgwd Clun-gwyn (Waterfall)
252
Fall
Nedd Fechan
Waterfall
262
Glyn-mercher-uchaf
Clyn-gwyn
258
Pen-y-ddeufryn
Heol Calch
Pont Melin-fach
90
91
92
Ford
Sgwd Isaf Clun-gwyn (Waterfall)
93
290
Waterfalls
Nantllechau
197
Glyn-mercher-isaf
258
Sgwd y Pannwr (Waterfall)
270
Waterfall
250
10
Scwd Ddwli (Waterfall)
249
Gwaen-goch-dimai
Comin y Rhos
Waterfall
Waterfalls
Sgwd yr Eira (Waterfall)
273
C861
240
Waterfalls
Sheepfold
Carn-y-crochan
Sheepfold
Cefn-d'rysgoed
Spr
230
Ws
Cilhepste-fach
Stepping Stones
Waterfall
Gwernblaedda
Glan-yr-afon
Pentre-d'rysgoed
Bryn-chwyth
220
Waterfall
Cilhepste-cerig
FB
E
Lletty-Dreffydd
CG
200
213
09
FB
Cwm Gored
Hendrefydd
Weir
Spr
Lluest
180
190
150
140
186
Chy
FB
325
Ffynnon Ddu (Spring)
159
Spr
Ford
Nant-y-celyn
Waterfall
Glyn Neath Golf Club
194
Clwyd-rhyd-fan
Craig y Ddinas
Mine
CH
08
Spr
Pontneddfechan
Farm
PC
FB
Coed y Ffyrnau
Pen-cae-drain
Ynys-cambwll
Waterfall
260
Cambwll
A465
240
B4242
77
Wks
Coed Wernhir
Tyle-morgrug
200
Spr

Sgwd Ddwli on the Afon Nedd Fechan

waymarked stile confirming the public footpath. The clear path undulates high above the Nedd Fechan, crossing two more stiles and numerous side streams to reach the bridge at Pont Rhyd-y-cnau G.

Here turn right at the footpath sign to Gwaun Bryn-bwch, along a track winding steadily uphill through woodland. Emerging from the trees, continue uphill and go through a metal gate onto a lane. Turn right along the lane, which bends right to a T-junction. Turn left and after a few yards bear right H. At a blue-waymarked post turn left off the track, go through a wooden gate and downhill along an enclosed path, passing through a series of gates to reach the road opposite the car park at the start.

Fan y Big

Start	Torpantau
Distance	10 miles (16.1km)
Height gain	2,000 feet (610m)
Approximate time	5½ hours
Parking	Forestry Commission Upper Waterfalls free car park at Torpantau
Route terrain	Mainly clear paths over high mountains. Some steep going. Easy return along a broad track and quiet lane
Ordnance Survey maps	Landranger 160 (Brecon Beacons), Explorer OL12 (Brecon Beacons National Park – Western area)

GPS waypoints

Start	SO 056 175
A	SO 057 205
B	SO 036 206
C	SO 031 205
D	SO 033 181
E	SO 035 173
F	SO 049 167

After an initial steep climb, the rest of this walk in the heart of the Brecon Beacons is relatively relaxing. The climb is to the ridges of Craig y Fan Ddu and later Graig Fan Las, which the walk follows to reach the main north-facing escarpment of the Beacons. After a dramatic stretch along the curving rim of the escarpment to the summit of Fan y Big, the route descends to the 'Gap Road' and follows this trackway, which is thought to be Roman, above the Neuadd reservoirs. Finally there is a pleasant, scenic stroll along the Taff Trail through the woodlands of Taf Fechan Forest. Although this is a comparatively easy mountain walk, much of it is along the edge of steep escarpments and therefore do not attempt it in winter or in misty weather unless properly experienced and equipped for such conditions.

Begin by walking back to the car park entrance and crossing a cattle-grid before turning right onto an uphill path, by a wire fence on the right and above a stream and waterfalls on the left. Follow the wire fence as it curves round to the right and after it ends keep straight ahead, more steeply uphill, to reach a cairn at the top of the ridge. To the right there are superb views over the Talybont valley to the long ridges of the Black Mountains on the horizon.

Continue along the well-surfaced path that runs along the ridge top of Craig y fan Ddu with the impressive, sweeping, smooth curve of the ridge of Graig Fan Las ahead. Later bear right to ford a stream and continue, curving gradually right along Graig Fan Las and enjoying the magnificent open, empty views to the right over mountain and forest. When you eventually reach the main escarpment of the Brecon Beacons turn sharp left A.

Keep along the clear, well-used path to the summit of Fan y Big, following the edge of the escarpment as it bends left and later curves right around the head of the valley of Cwm Oergwm. This is a typical Beacons landscape of sweeping, bare, smooth curves, steep escarpments, flat summits and wide vistas, with views beyond of the gentler scenery of the Usk Valley and the houses of Brecon. On reaching Fan y Big's rather unremarkable summit **B** turn sharp left, still walking along the edge of the escarpment, to descend into the broad col of Bwlch ar y Fan which lies between Fan y Big and Cribyn. Ahead looms the abrupt and daunting-looking peak of Cribyn, to the left the Upper Neuadd Reservoir can be seen and to the right there is a view down Cwm Cynwyn to the Usk Valley.

At the col turn left **C** along a broad, flat, stony track, which is thought to be of Roman origin and is usually referred to as the 'Gap Road' because it makes use of the gap in the escarpment. Follow this trackway above the Upper Neuadd Reservoir and after 1½ miles, where the main track turns right **D**, there is a choice of routes. *If the stream below is fordable, bear left and head steeply down a rocky track to ford it, head up the other side and continue along the right-hand edge of conifers to descend gently to a road. Otherwise, follow the main track to the right down to a metal gate, turn left onto a path in front of it, cross the stream, climb a stile and continue along the road ahead.* The track and road meet at a junction **E**, where you should turn left to take the track ahead, which is part of the Taff Trail. It runs to the left of the road, by a wire fence on the right and along the edge of the conifers of Taf Fechan Forest. Ahead are most attractive views towards Talybont reservoir. The track passes through several gates and continues through woodland, eventually bending right to cross a stream and rejoin the road **F**. Turn left and follow the road uphill for just over ½ mile to return to the starting point.

On the escarpment of the Brecon Beacons

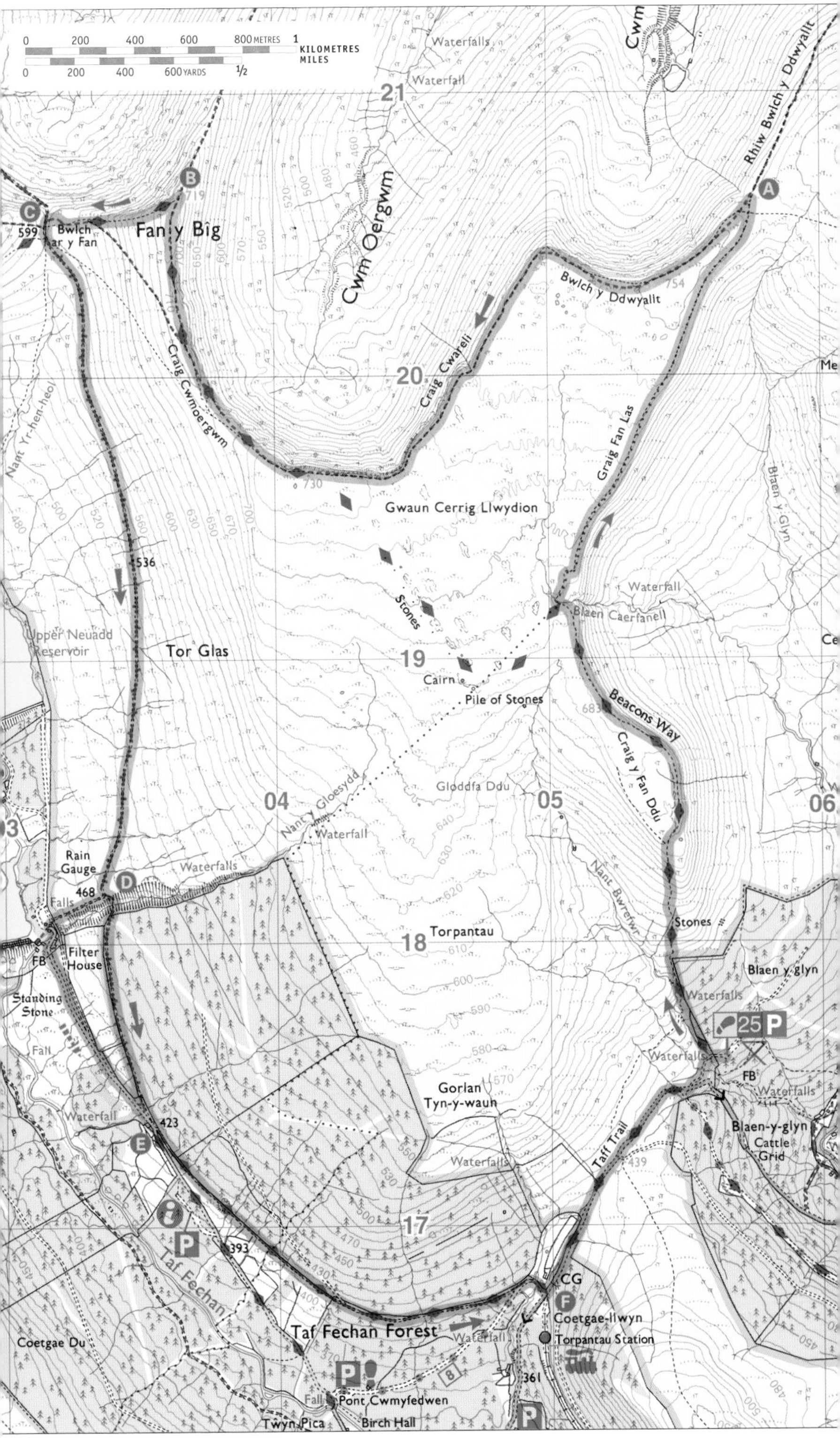
0 200 400 600 800 METRES 1 KILOMETRES
MILES
0 200 400 600 YARDS 1/2
Waterfalls
Waterfall
Cwm
Rhiw Bwlch y Ddwyallt
Fan y Bîg
Bwlch ar y Fan
Cwm Oergwm
Bwlch y Ddwyallt
Craig Cwareli
Craig Cwmoergwm
Craig Fan Las
Nant Yr-hen-heol
Gwaun Cerrig Llwydion
Blaen y Glyn
Stones
Blaen Caerfanell
Upper Neuadd Reservoir
Tor Glas
Cairn
Pile of Stones
Beacons Way
Craig y Fan Ddu
Nant y Gloesydd
Gloddfa Ddu
Rain Gauge
Waterfalls
Nant Bwrefwr
Falls
Filter House
Torpantau
Stones
Blaen y glyn
Standing Stone
Fall
Gorlan Tyn-y-waun
FB
Blaen-y-glyn
Cattle Grid
Taff Trail
Taf Fechan
CG
Coetgae-llwyn
Torpantau Station
Taf Fechan Forest
Coetgae Du
Pont Cwmyfedwen
Twyn Pica
Birch Hall

Waun Fach

		GPS waypoints
Start	Pengenffordd	SO 173 296
Distance	7 miles (11.3km)	Ⓐ SO 178 301
Height gain	2,200 feet (670m)	Ⓑ SO 195 310
Approximate time	4½ hours	Ⓒ SO 212 308
Parking	Castle Inn car park (pay in the pub)	Ⓓ SO 215 299
Route terrain	Clear and often boggy paths over high mountains and open moorland. *Navigation would be difficult in poor visibility*	Ⓔ SO 204 286
Ordnance Survey maps	Landranger 161 (The Black Mountains), Explorer OL13 (Brecon Beacons National Park – Eastern area)	Ⓕ SO 186 289

After a short, steep climb at the start of the walk to the scanty remains of Castell Dinas, a magnificent viewpoint, the rest of the route to the 2,660 ft (810m) summit of Waun Fach, the highest point in the Black Mountains, is a lengthy and steady rather than strenuous ascent, much of which involves an exhilarating ramble along a switchback ridge. Route-finding could be difficult and potentially hazardous in bad weather, especially misty conditions, therefore save this walk for a fine day when the extensive views can be enjoyed to the full.

Head down the set of wooden steps at the back of the car park and turn right onto a rough track. Follow this for a few paces and then turn left, over a stile, onto a permissive path that leads to Castell Dinas. This drops steeply down to a small stream, which you cross, before making your way up the steep left-hand edge of the field on the other side. Continue, all the time on the same line until you reach the lower ramparts of Castell Dinas, a Norman Castle built on the original site of an Iron Age Hill Fort Ⓐ. There's nothing much left of the castle but it's a great spot with views in all directions, including straight ahead along the full length of Y Grib, which rises like a dragon's back from the deep saddle at your feet.

Drop steeply into the saddle, cross the track that runs across it, and then climb up onto the ridge, ahead. Now simply follow the crest upwards on an easy path that vaults a few small rocky outcrops along the way. A small cairn marks a subsidiary top at 1,607 feet (490m), and beyond this, the path drops into a pronounced saddle named Bwlch Bach a'r Grîb – which translates to the 'Small Gap in the Ridge'. Climb steeply away from this and enjoy a lovely level section that leads to a final steep climb over a succession of small rocky steps.

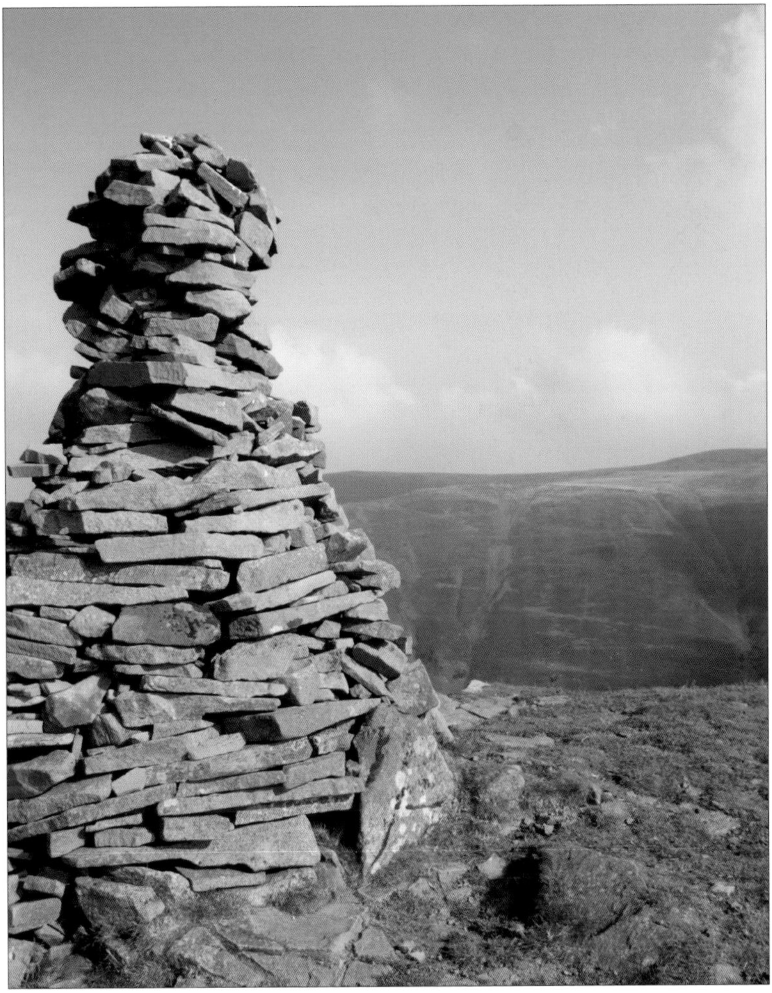

Cairn on Y Grib

Keep ahead the whole time, sticking to the crest as much as possible, until you eventually reach the magnificent cairn that crowns the true top of the ridge B.

Keep straight ahead crossing a broad plateau and then climbing steeply on a fainter path that eventually leads onto the main Black Mountains ridge, just a short distance north of the outlying summit of Pen y Manllwyn. Bear right onto a broad peaty path that leads to this summit, marked with a small cairn C, and then continue in the same direction to climb steadily, through a succession of peat hags, to the obvious summit of Waun Fach – marked by a plinth that once carried a trig point D. This is the highest point in the Black Mountains but it does not offer much in the way of views or shelter so it's probably best to keep moving.

Bear right to leave the boggy hollow and locate another peaty path that runs easily along a broad ridge with the Grwyne Fechan Valley dropping steeply away to the left. Follow this path easily around the head of the valley to the small summit of Pen Trumau, where it then drops steeply into a huge, deep saddle that's marked by large cairns E.

View towards Pen y Manllwyn from Waun Fach

This is a fabulous viewpoint and by far the best place to appreciate the real size and stature of Waun Fach as well as its twin peak, Pen y Gadair Fawr, which has a much more distinctive outline despite being slightly lower.

Turn right to drop down from the cairns and then keep left at a fork after 200 yds. The

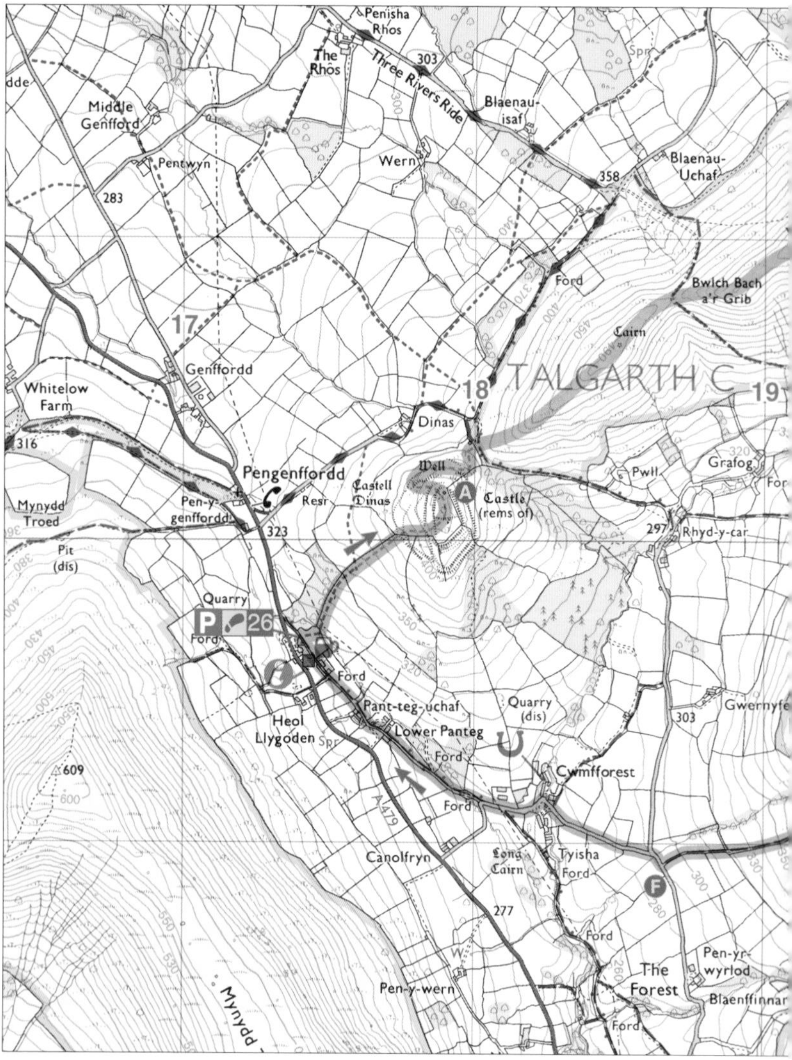

rough path now leads steeply down through sheep pasture, finally leaving the open moorland at a gate and dropping, between dry stone walls to a road F. Turn right and then left to drop steeply down to a bridge over the Afon Rhiangoll and then climb up the other side, where you'll see a rocky track leading off to the right, on a sharp left-hand bend. Take this and follow it for ½ mile, past the stile that you crossed at the start and back up the steps to the car park.

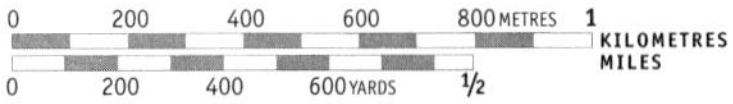

SCALE 1:25 000 or 2½ INCHES to 1 MILE *4CM to 1KM*

Craig-y-nos, Cribarth and the Henrhyd Falls

Start	Craig-y-nos Country Park
Distance	8½ miles (13.7km)
Height gain	1,935 feet (590m)
Approximate time	4½ hours
Parking	Pay and Display car park
Route terrain	A true mix of paths that cross mountains and woods. Some sections may be awkward in poor visibility. Some short sections of road walking and one longer stretch of quiet lane
Ordnance Survey maps	Landranger 160 (Brecon Beacons), Explorer OL12 (Brecon Beacons National Park – Western area)

GPS waypoints

Start	SN 839 155
A	SN 828 141
B	SN 829 133
C	SN 829 125
D	SN 834 126
E	SN 854 120
F	SN 851 124
G	SN 847 129
H	SN 848 147
J	SN 843 157

Craig-y-nos Country Park, formerly the grounds of a large house, is the starting point for this lengthy and unusually varied walk in Glyn Tawe, the upper reaches of the Swansea Valley on the southern fringes of the Black Mountain. The walk includes open hillside, a summit, woodland, riverside, a narrow ravine and the highest waterfall in South Wales, as well as having the historic interest of Craig-y-nos and the former quarrying activities in the area. In addition to being lengthy, this is quite an energetic walk with several ascents and descents but well worthwhile for the superb views and scenic contrasts.

In 1878 the tempestuous, internationally famous opera singer Adelina Patti fell in love with the romantic setting of Craig-y-nos Castle in the upper Swansea valley and the following year she bought it. Over the next 12 years she enlarged and modernised the early 19th-century castle and laid out over 40 acres of ornamental grounds. Such was her fame and wealth that at the nearby station she had her own railway carriage and a private waiting room for herself and her many distinguished visitors, who included the Prince of Wales, later Edward VII. After her death in 1919 the castle became a hospital and it is now a restaurant and function centre. In 1976 the grounds – woodland, meadow, lakes and river – were acquired by the Brecon Beacons National Park and restored as a country park.

Park at Craig-y-nos Country Park. Turn left on to the main road and follow it for about 400 yds passing in front of the 19th-century castle buildings and the coach house. Continue to a gate on the right, opposite a lay-by on the left, and pass through it to follow the grassy track uphill, signed to the open hill. Bear sharp right after a few paces and follow the narrow track up the steep hillside in a series of zigzags, that are marked with white-topped posts. Turn left on reaching the fence at the top, and keep this to your right to continue climbing steeply to a stile over a wall.

Climb the stile and turn right to follow the wall up over the side of the limestone crag, then down past a stile to a gate in the wall on the right. Turn left to follow a faint path easily upwards passing through a natural amphitheatre with a rock-covered hillside directly ahead. Keep right near the top, to locate a clearer path, and then follow this leftwards, in front of the rock-strewn hill, to meet a clearer, grassy, quarry track. Turn right onto this and continue around the hillside for a few paces, meeting a wall on the left. The triangulation pillar on the summit of Cribarth 1,390 feet (423m) can be seen ahead; bear right and head up to it Ⓐ for the magnificent all-round view that takes in the hilly moorlands of Fforest Fawr, almost the whole length of the Swansea valley, the hills that guard the northern end of the former mining valleys and the barren, empty wilderness of the Black Mountain.

From the summit keep straight ahead to wind your way between outcrops and back down to the original track, which should be followed downhill, with a wall on the left. At a wall corner a disused quarry tramroad can be seen contouring along the side of the hill ahead but at this point you turn left and make your way between boulders to a stile and footpath sign about 50 yds ahead. Climb the stile and, following the direction of a yellow waymark to the right, continue along a grassy path that contours around the slopes of Cribarth, keeping parallel to a wall and a wire fence on the right.

The path gradually bears left following the curve of the hill and heads down to a short marker post, and beyond that to a stile. Do not climb over the stile but instead turn left, in the direction of a public footpath sign to Ynyswen, and continue through rocks, bracken and heather along the southern flanks of Cribarth. Keep ahead at a junction of paths, marked by a wooden post, and cross a short boardwalk to a stile in the fence on the left. Cross this and keep ahead along the right-hand edge of the field to another stile. Cross this and turn right to go through a metal gate at the top of the woodland Ⓑ. Fork immediately right and descend through the beautiful, steep-sided Abercrave Wood to reach a metal gate in front of a barn.

Go through, keep ahead, pass through the right-hand one of two metal gates straight ahead and continue along a track by a stream on the right. Keep to the right of farm buildings and then turn right along a tarmac drive. At a junction by the **Abercrave Inn** turn sharp left down a road and take the first turning on the right along a road that first bends sharply to the right and then turns left to cross a bridge over the River Tawe.

On the other side of the bridge turn left at a public footpath sign, go through a kissing-gate to the left of a house and continue along a tarmac path beside the river. Go through a second kissing-gate, pass under a road, go through a third one and keep ahead to a footpath sign. Turn left to keep alongside the river, below sloping woodland, and a few yards farther on follow the direction of a waymarked post to bear slightly right uphill and continue through woodland above the river. Head up to keep by a hedge bank and line of trees on the right, climb a stile, continue along the left-hand edge of a field, above the top edge of the wood and by a wire fence on the left, and climb another stile onto a lane C.

Turn left along the lane for nearly ½ mile, keep left at a fork, descend steeply and follow the lane around a right-hand bend to Llech Bridge. Cross the bridge, continue along the lane for about 50 yds and at a public footpath sign turn right over a stile D. There is now an attractive stretch along an undulating path by the side of the beautiful gorge of the River Llech to the Henrhyd Falls. The path is mostly high up above the river, with steps in places and several stiles and footbridges. Approaching the falls the route continues by bearing left along an uphill path, but for a better view keep ahead, turn right over a footbridge and turn left to continue to the impressive falls which at just under 100 feet (30m) are the highest in South Wales. They are now owned by the National Trust. Retrace your steps to take the steep uphill path, go through two gates at the top and continue through a car park to a road E. Turn left along the road (or to visit the pub, turn right over the bridge) and keep ahead for nearly ½ mile.

At a left-hand bend by a mast F *there is a choice of routes. If you would prefer to avoid a stretch of boggy walking (for instance after wet weather), go round the left-hand bend and continue for just under ½ mile until you reach a road leading off to the right. Go down this, and after about ¼ mile and two slight bends to the right you rejoin the main route at* G *below.*

If you don't mind covering boggy ground, climb the stile at F and keep ahead – there is no obvious path – across an area of rough pasture, bearing slightly left and heading down to cross a footbridge. Continue in the same direction to a stile, climb it and head gently uphill towards the right-hand edge of the line of trees in front. Here bear right alongside a fence on the left, go through a gap in a wire fence ahead and, keeping by a hedge bank and fence on the left, bear left and head downhill by a stream on the right.

Climb a stile onto a lane G, turn right over a bridge and follow the lane for ½ mile, heading downhill. There are superb views of Cribarth and along the Tawe Valley to the prominent Carmarthen Fans on the skyline. Where the lane turns left to cross Pen-y-cae Bridge keep ahead, at a public bridleway sign, along a tarmac drive. In front of a metal gate fork left onto an enclosed, tree-lined path and continue to a lane. Keep ahead along the lane, which later joins a wider one.

Just after passing an outdoor centre on the right, bear left H along a tarmac, hedge-lined track. Where this ends in front of a farm bear left again through a metal gate, passing to the left of the farm-house, and continue along an enclosed path. Later the path keeps along the right-hand edge of woodland, by a wire fence on the left and below

steep rocky slopes on the right. At a fork **J**, go left through a wooden gate and drop to a bridge over the River Tawe. Do not cross but instead turn left, with the river to your right, and walk easily along the banks, through trees, to a bridge on the right. Cross this and bear right then left at the pond, to return to the start.

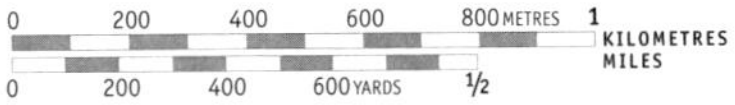

Brecon Beacons Horseshoe

Start	Cwm Gwdi
Distance	8½ miles (13.7km)
Height gain	2,890 feet (880m)
Approximate time	5 hours
Parking	Free car park in Cwm Gwdi
Route terrain	Mainly good paths over high mountains but one short untracked section and some steep climbs and drops. The return leg follows quiet, narrow lanes
Ordnance Survey maps	Landranger 160 (Brecon Beacons), Explorer OL12 (Brecon Beacons National Park – Western area)

GPS waypoints

Start	SO 023 247
A	SO 032 244
B	SO 023 222
C	SO 023 213
D	SO 011 215
E	SO 007 213
F	SO 011 252

This walk, which includes the three main peaks of the Brecon Beacons, is arguably the finest mountain walk in South Wales and one of the best in the country. A lengthy, gradual, steadily ascending approach leads to the foot of Cribyn, then the final climb up to its summit (2,608ft/795m) is steep and exhausting. A descent into a col is followed by another steep, though short, pull up to Pen y Fan (2,907ft/886m), the highest point in the Brecon Beacons and the highest point in Britain south of Snowdonia. A much gentler descent and ascent leads onto the distinctive flat summit of Corn Du (2,863ft 873m). The return route drops down to the beautiful little lake of Llyn Cwm Llwch, and this is followed by a relaxing stroll through the lovely valley of Cwm Llwch. This is a walk worth taking plenty of time over; the approach and return are every bit as enjoyable as the three peaks themselves and the views are magnificent. But do not attempt it in poor, especially misty, weather, unless experienced in such conditions and able to use a compass.

Begin by walking down a muddy path that leads left out of the top car park. Cross a stile on the right and a footbridge over the Nant Gwdi. Turn right to follow the path up through scrubby woodland, with the brook to the right, and keep heading up until you emerge from the trees onto an open hillside. Bear left to contour around the hillside, keeping the steep bracken covered slopes to your right, and the wooded lower slopes to your left. Continue around until you see a gate down to your left **A**, and trend rightwards to follow a clear path up into Cwm Sere, with fantastic views up the valley to Cribyn and Pen y Fan.

Follow this path effortlessly up the

valley for about $1\frac{1}{2}$ miles, until the path gradually drops to meet the Nant Sere above some waterfalls **B**. Cross the stream above the falls, and make your way directly up the steep hillside beyond. Continue climbing to the top, where you'll meet a good path that runs along Bryn Teg. Turn right onto this and climb easily at first, and then steeply, to the summit of Cribyn **C**. The reward is a magnificent view which includes Fan y Big, the Black Mountains, Llangorse Lake, Brecon, the Usk Valley, the hills of mid Wales, Pen y Fan, Corn Du and the peaks and reservoirs to the south.

Turn right and make for the summit of Pen y Fan along a clear, broad, path, heading steeply down into a col and equally steeply uphill again, with a final, rocky scramble to the cairn that marks the summit **D**. From here there is an even more spectacular view because it includes Fforest Fawr and the Black Mountain to the west and the beautiful little lake of Llyn Cwm Llwch below. Now bear left and make your way to the third of the trio of summits, the flat-topped Corn Du – thankfully there is only a modest descent and ascent this time.

From the summit cairn on Corn Du **E** keep in the same direction and after an initial steep descent turn right to continue along the edge of the escarpment above Llyn Cwm Llwch. The memorial passed by is to Tommy Jones, a five-year-old boy whose body was found here in 1900. He was visiting his grandparents who lived in Cwm Llwch, and became separated from his father as they walked from the rail station in Brecon. The obelisk was moved slightly a few years ago to try and stem the erosion that surrounded it. Shortly after the monument follow the path that descends quite steeply towards the left-hand side of the lake. From this path there are spectacular views of the great natural amphitheatre formed by Corn

Pen y fan – the highest point in southern Britain

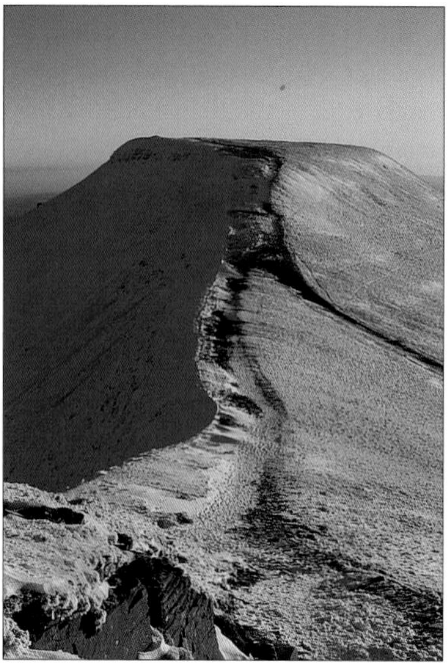

Pen y fan in winter

Du and Pen y Fan that encloses the lake, and of the lovely green valley of Cwm Llwch with Brecon and the gentler landscapes of the Usk Valley beyond.

Upon reaching the outlet of Llyny Cwm Llwch bear slightly left to continue through the valley, keeping to the left of the stream all the way. This is an outstandingly attractive and relaxing section of the walk; the path is clear and easy to follow and there are constant superb views. At first you head fairly gently downhill across open grassland to climb a stile by a National Trust sign for Cwm Llwch. Then continue through the increasingly more gentle and wooded terrain and just in front of a cottage turn left over a waymarked stile. Turn right to climb another one, keep ahead by a wall on the right, and soon after the wall ends curve first to the right and then turn left to continue along a delightful, tree-lined track enclosed by low walls, with the stream close by.

Climb a stile, then cross a footbridge over a tributary stream and continue beside the stream to a parking area. Pass through it, go through a metal gate and

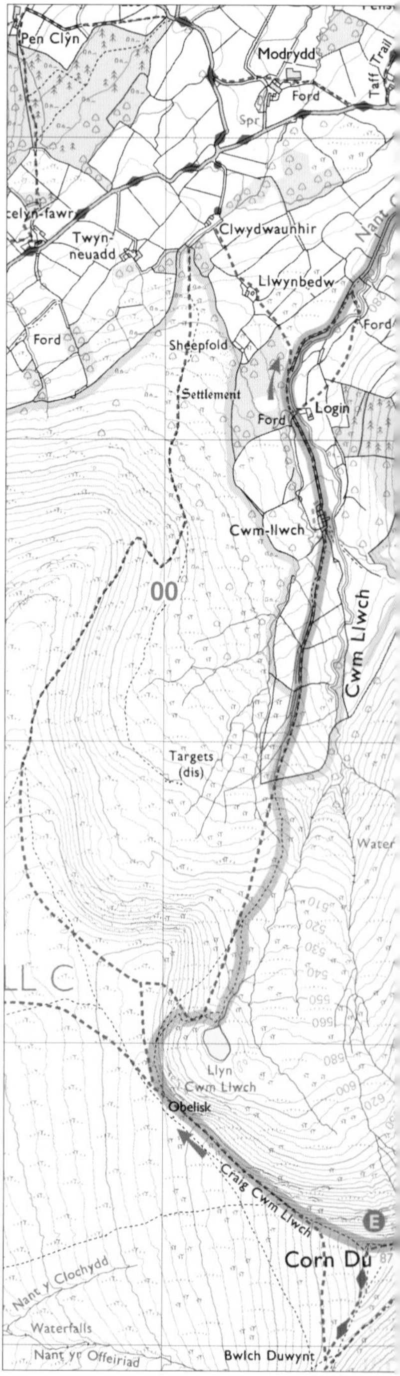

continue along the track ahead, which soon becomes a tarmac track. At a crossroads turn right F, cross the stream and follow a narrow lane for 1 mile, keeping ahead at a junction, to the entrance to Cwm Gwdi Training Camp. Turn right through the entrance to return to the start.

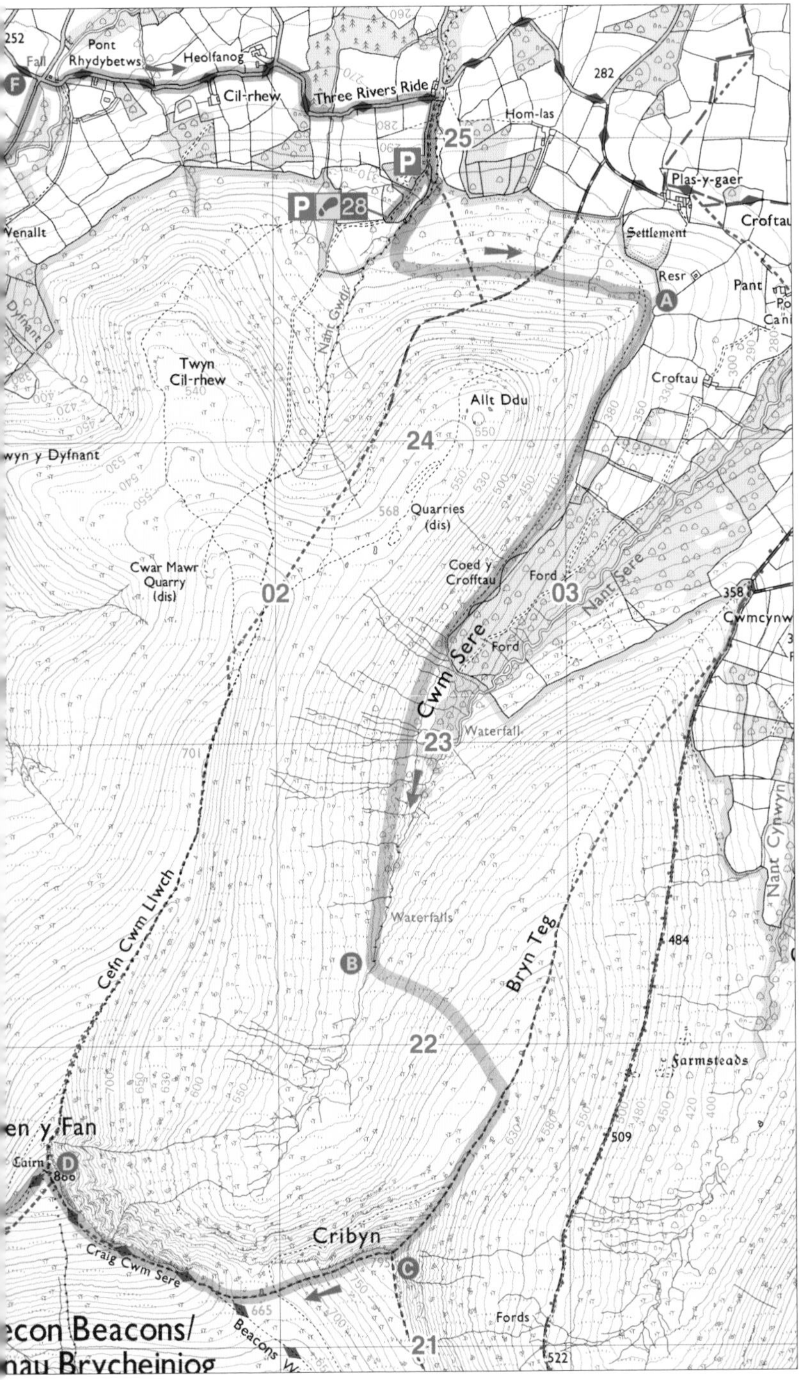

SCALE 1:25000 or 2½ INCHES to 1 MILE *4CM to 1KM*

Further Information

Safety on the Hills

The hills, mountains and moorlands of Britain, though of modest height compared with those in many other countries, need to be treated with respect. Friendly and inviting in good weather, they can quickly be transformed into wet, misty, windswept and potentially dangerous areas of wilderness in bad weather. Even on an outwardly fine and settled summer day, conditions can rapidly deteriorate at high altitudes and, in winter, even more so.

Therefore it is advisable to always take both warm and waterproof clothing, sufficient nourishing food, a hot drink, first-aid kit, torch and whistle. Wear suitable footwear, such as strong walking boots or shoes that give a good grip over rocky terrain and on slippery slopes. Try to obtain a local weather forecast and bear it in mind before you start. Do not be afraid to abandon your proposed route and return to your starting point in the event of a sudden and unexpected deterioration in the weather. Do not go alone and allow enough time to finish the walk well before nightfall.

Most of the walks described in this book do not venture into remote wilderness areas and will be safe to do, given due care and respect, at any time of year in all but the most unreasonable weather. Indeed, a crisp, fine winter day often provides perfect walking conditions, with firm ground underfoot and a clarity that is not possible to achieve in the other seasons of the year. A few walks, however, are suitable only for reasonably fit and experienced hill walkers able to use a compass and should definitely not be tackled by anyone else during the winter months or in bad weather, especially high winds and mist. These are indicated in the general description that precedes each of the walks.

Walkers and the Law

The Countryside and Rights of Way Act (CRoW Act 2000) extends the rights of access previously enjoyed by walkers in England and Wales. Implementation of these rights began on 19 September 2004. The Act amends existing legislation and for the first time provides access on foot to certain types of land – defined as mountain, moor, heath, down and registered common land.

Where You Can Go

Rights of Way

Prior to the introduction of the CRoW Act, walkers could only legally access the countryside along public rights of way. These are either 'footpaths' (for walkers only) or 'bridleways' (for walkers, riders on horseback and pedal cyclists). A third category called 'Byways open to all traffic' (BOATs), is used by motorised vehicles as well as those using non-mechanised transport. Mainly they are green lanes, farm and estate roads, although occasionally they will be found crossing mountainous area.

Rights of way are marked on Ordnance Survey maps. Look for the green broken lines on the Explorer maps, or the red dashed lines on Landranger maps.

The term 'right of way' means exactly what it says. It gives a right of passage over what, for the most part, is private land. Under pre-CRoW legislation walkers were required to keep to the line of the right of way and not stray onto land on either side. If you did inadvertently wander off the right of way, either because of faulty map reading or because the route was not clearly indicated on the ground, you were technically trespassing.

Local authorities have a legal obligation to ensure that rights of way are kept clear and free of obstruction, and are signposted where they leave metalled roads. The duty of local authorities to install signposts